Using Dignities
in
Astrology

Charles Obert

Almuten Press

Minneapolis, Minnesota

2018

Published and printed in the United States of America

By Almuten Press

3507 Taylor Street NE, Minneapolis, MN 55418

http://studentofastrology.com

©2018 by Charles Obert

ISBN-13: 978-0-9864187-1-6

A PDF version of this book is available for purchase at the author's website,

http://studentofastrology.com

Dedication

To Enid Newberg and Karen McCauley at Kepler College.

Acknowledgements

I want to thank all of the students in my dignities class at Kepler College for their wonderful insights, questions and feedback. They did more to shape this book than they realize.

Special thanks to Rebecca Bihr, Estelle Daniels, Maddie Youngstrom, Denise Menton and Shea Steeples for their feedback on earlier versions of this book.

Also by Charles Obert

_____

Introduction to Traditional Natal Astrology: A Complete Working Guide for Modern Astrologers (2015)
(Available in print through standard retail outlets,
and in PDF form at the website, http://studentofastrology.com)

Forthcoming

_____

Directions Through the Bounds in Traditional Astrology
(projected late 2018)

Astrology and Platonic Philosophy
(projected 2019)

For further information on these publications, and other projects by the author, please visit the website,

http://studentofastrology.com

Table of Contents

Purpose

This book started with my experience leading a traditional astrology study group for several years. The members of that group included my teacher and friend Ben Dykes, and the fine traditional astrologer Estelle Daniels. Among the regular participants were the fine modern astrologers Shawn Nygaard and Maddie Youngstrom. I learned a great deal from all of them, and I am grateful to have been in a study group with them.

The book came to fruition teaching classes on dignities at Kepler College, beginning in early 2016. I learned a lot from my students with their different backgrounds and perspectives.

These are my goals in writing this book.

First, I want to present a systematic way to use dignity and debility to evaluate the strengths and weaknesses of a chart. Some of this material is covered in my first book, *Introduction to Traditional Natal Astrology*. In this new book I am going into much further detail, especially with the minor dignities. You can view this new work as a greatly expanded version of a portion of my first book.

I particularly want to recover using the minor dignities, each of which has its own distinct flavor and function.

For all of the dignities I want to offer more concrete metaphors to make interpretation less abstract and more specific.

These techniques originated with traditional astrology, and at this point they are mainly practiced by those who consider themselves traditional. I want to change that. I think that these techniques are just as useful when used in a modern psychological astrology context.

I am convinced that the dignity and debility system is the heart of astrology, and in this book I want to show you how to use the system to deepen your current practice.

Introduction

In this introduction I want to provide a context for understanding dignity and debility.

Dignities at the Heart of Astrology

The practice of traditional astrology originally developed to answer specific questions - questions like the following.

Will my infant child live?
Will I be healthy?
Will I marry, and if so, what quality will it be?
Will I be rich or poor?
What is a good time to get married?

Given a specific question like that, the tools of traditional astrology are used to go into the chart, find the planets and houses that are related to the question being asked, and determine their condition. If the planets in question are in good shape, that area of the person's life will likely go well. If the planets are in bad shape, that area of life is likely to be a disappointment or a source of difficulty.

You weigh up the preponderance of fortunate or unfortunate indicators for the chosen topic, and judge accordingly.

When you do general chart evaluation, as in much modern practice, evaluation of the location and natures of the planets gives information on which areas of life the good or ill fortune will be, which areas are likely to go smoothly, and which areas are likely to take a lot of work or struggle or challenge. If there is a problem area in the chart, the system of dignities can give useful information as to how to deal with it, how to work with it - and, sometimes, how to turn a challenge into an asset - not always, but sometimes.

The very heart of astrology involves weighing up the parts of a chart
For relative strength and condition,
balance and imbalance.
The heart of weighing up a chart
is the system of essential and accidental dignities.

The use of the evaluation techniques of dignity and debility have been largely lost in much of modern astrology. In this book I want to restore them to their central and important place.

Concrete and Rich Meaning

Over the centuries, the use of the terms for dignity and debility have lost much of their meaning. They have become black and white abstractions, up and down tick marks on a planetary score sheet. In this book we will look at recovering much of the original richness of meaning of the language. We will flesh out the terms for the different kinds of dignity and debility and make their meanings more colorful, concrete, sensual and rich.

In order to do that, we need to get past thinking in terms of good and bad opposites. We will look at how opposites are used, in our astrology, and in our thinking in general.

Concepts of Opposites and Cycles

I want to start this section by contrasting the world of astrology with our modern way of thinking of the world.

The Shape of Our World

Astrology looks at the world in terms of cycles, ascending and descending waves, and complementary opposites. The shape of astrology is cyclical, circular, wavelike.

By contrast, our modern world thinks of reality in single direction straight lines, and in polarized opposites.

The world around us behaves in ways that match the shape of astrology, with cycles of growth and decay. Meanwhile in much of our culture we are thinking in terms of straight lines, and this can cause problems.

When the shape of our thinking mismatches the shape of the world around us we get ourselves in trouble.

Consider this graph of a wave.

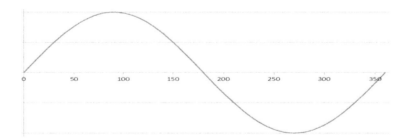

The wave is a good metaphor for cycles of growth and change. It is a map of the four seasons, with the equinoxes being where the graph cuts the center line, and the solstices being the peak or valley of each curve. It is a map of the Sun's distance above or below the equator during its yearly journey. It is a map of the daily cycle of day and night.

This cyclical shape also maps a living organism's life span, including birth, growth, flourishing, decline, decay and death, with the possibility of rebirth in a new form.

It maps the life of collective organisms like a family, a business, a city, a country, a church, an economy, or a civilization. It maps cyclical processes like a career or a job.

In this next illustration we have the same sine wave with a straight line mapped on top of it. The wave and the line start out aligned, but then increasingly diverge.

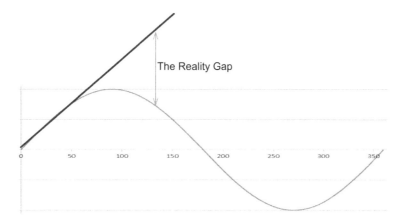

The curved line shows the cyclical astrology view of the world, and the straight line shows how much of our modern thinking works.

Straight line thinking works just fine where the line overlaps the wave and the cycle is on the up curve. It works great while you're young, you're growing, you're prosperous – when things are "looking up". However, as the two graphs get increasingly out of sync, the straight line model of the world becomes increasingly dysfunctional.

That increasing mismatch between the wave reality, and the straight line perception of it, is a Reality Gap.

In a straight line model of the world we have no good way of dealing with the peak and decline part of the sine wave. We don't recognize it when it happens so we have no strategy to deal with it. Faced with the decline we tend to take actions to keep the line going straight and up. The further out of sync the two lines become, the more we are setting ourselves up for a correction to re-align them.

If we can't think about something then we have no way to deal with it. It is off our radar.

This straight line model corresponds to a use of astrology that looks for everything to be positive, and for there to be perpetual growth, progress and improvement. Our experience is much more complex than that, including ups and downs, easy and difficult areas, good and bad fortune. Our astrology needs to include that complexity and change.

Pairs of Opposites

Our experience is an expression of cycles of the interaction of complementary opposites in a dance of transformation, and the symbolism of astrology is structured in terms of these opposites.

There is Day and Night, Light and Darkness, the most primal of opposites. Neither lasts forever, each gradually turns into the other, and there are phases of light and darkness within the daily cycle.

To label dawn as good and twilight as evil is silly - *about as silly as labeling birth good, and death, evil - or, labeling childhood and youth good, and old age evil.*

These different shapes effect how we think about opposites. In a straight line model of reality the opposites are the two ends of a straight line, and the ends are antagonistic and enemies. The ends of a straight line never meet.

Consider another image, where the line turns back on itself. This is the wheel of complementary opposites called Tai Chi, also called Yin and Yang. Picture the Tai Chi symbol rolling forward like a ball, unfolding over time, and it maps to the graph of the wave. The wave and the wheel are two different images for the same process.

In contrast with the straight line model, in a wave model the opposites are complementary and balancing, and succeed each other through a cycle of time. The opposites get to an extreme, and then turn around and transform into the other.

Extreme Yang becomes Yin, extreme Yin becomes Yang. Winter reaches an extreme of cold then moves towards spring heat, and Summer reaches an extreme of heat and moves towards Autumn and cold. The opposites continually transform into each other.

Instead of labeling opposites as adversaries, this model views them as complementary parts of an ongoing cycle, each necessary and appropriate in its own way.

This gives us a way to think about the concepts of dignity and debility that avoids labeling them good and evil.

Astrology and the Opposites

There is day and night, there is feminine and masculine. They have different qualities and both are needed.

There is also benefic and malefic, dignity and debility. They also have different qualities, and both are needed.

In our modern world, we tend to emphasize only the parts of the cycle that we view as desirable, and try to deny or hide the parts we don't want to deal with. We view growth and increase as desirable, while decrease and decline are not so good even to admit.

Birth is a joyous event, and death is a tragedy to be fought as long as possible. Youth is considered good, while aging with its loss of strength and beauty is evil and to be denied.

We value one half of the cycle, and deny or fight the balancing half. We do not have a sense of the worth, usefulness or necessity of decline as well as growth, of death as well as birth. Each is useful and necessary in its place. In our astrology we need to allow a place for both, and the paired concepts connected to dignity and debility are part of how we can describe and mirror the process.

Accepting Change

You never step in the same river twice. - Heraclitus

In our human experience here on earth there is no permanence. Everything in our experience goes through the process of being born, growing, changing, declining and dying, then being reborn in a new form. This applies to to people, to societies, cultures, countries, and civilizations. No created being is exempt from the cycle of birth and death.

Within society, some people are on the way up, and some on the way down. Some are highly respected, some are despised and ignored. And, no-one stays at one place in the cycle forever. Today's in group is tomorrow's out group.

The major dignities, which we examine in detail in the next section, relate to these same cyclic pairs. There is rulership and detriment, and there is exaltation and fall. Think of them as phases in a cycle rather than as good and bad. Each has its place and its usefulness.

Balance and Unbalance

A condition of overall balance is a desirable state. Such a state of balance, harmony, and ease is related to the concept of dignity. A difficult state is off-balance, tense, extreme, and out of harmony, and this is related to debility.

In isolation, it seems at first glance that balance and harmony is desirable, and unbalance and disharmony are undesirable. Yet, as you move through time, the off-balance and extreme states are necessary to keep the overall system healthy and balanced, to keep it from growing stale and lifeless. A mix of balance and imbalance is part of the cycle of growth and change.

Balance in Time

Dignity and debility are not static concepts. Since each relates to a cycle of change, there are appropriate places for each. Being in balance also includes being in harmony with the surrounding cycles of change.

Even within overall balance there is a need for unbalanced force in order for things to change. To birth something new means to allow something old to lose its form and die. Dignity has its place and purpose, and so does debility.

Keep this key concept of balance within a cycle in mind as we approach the concepts of dignity and debility. A planet in its dignity serves a purpose, a planet in its debility serves another purpose, and each is necessary and appropriate in its place.

A Note on House Systems

I use two different house systems in my practice. My primary system is Whole Sign, where the entire zodiac sign where the Ascendant falls is the first house, and each house is an entire sign. In this system the Midheaven can fall in a house other than the tenth - sometimes in the ninth or eleventh house, occasionally in the eighth or even the twelfth depending on latitude and time of day. Whole sign is probably the earliest house system we have on record.

There is another class called Quadrant house systems, in which the degree of the Ascendant marks the beginning of the first house, and the degree of the Midheaven marks the beginning of the tenth house. The other houses are determined by dividing up the quadrants between the Ascendant/Descendant and Midheaven/Immure Coeli axes. Different quadrant systems use different methods of dividing up the quadrants to get the intermediate house cusps. When I use a quadrant house system I typically use Placidus, which uses a time related calculation to determine house cusps. Deborah Houlding points out that, with Placidus houses, each house takes up two planetary hours of time.

In my practice I often draw up charts with both house systems, and I find the information from the two complement each other. If I had to choose just one I would go with Whole sign.

Almost all of the examples in this book use either Whole sign or Placidus, and the charts are labeled. The example charts from William Lilly use the Regiomontanus house system since that was Lilly's preferred choice.

Dignity and Debility

The terms dignity and debility are complex, and they have taken on a wide range of meanings throughout the history of astrology. I want to start our examination of dignity and debility by looking at the definitions and etymology of the terms. Our discussion will grow out of these meanings.

Dignity

The word dignity is from the Old French *dignite* meaning dignity, privilege, honor, and from Latin *dignitatem* meaning worthiness, from *dignus* meaning worthy, proper, fitting. This is related to the Latin root *decere* meaning proper or decent. The word includes the concepts of being worthy, privileged, fitting, acknowledged, having value.

The concept of dignity connotes a person being in the right place at the right time, a place where they belong and are acknowledged. It means being competent. It also includes a sense of recognized authority, so it includes respect or status.

Debility

By contrast, the connotations of the term debility are very different. Debility is from Middle French *debilite* or from Latin *debilitatem* meaning laming, crippling, weakening, from *debilis* meaning lame, disabled, crippled, and figuratively meaning weak and helpless. Debilis comes from de- "from, away" + -bilis, "strength", so moving away from strength, being weakened, lacking power.

The primary metaphor of the term debility is one of strength and weakness. Debility means being worn down, weakened or crippled. If dignity is powerful then debility is weak, decreases power or makes powerless. If dignity builds up then debility tears down. If dignity brings things together then debility tears apart.

Dignity speaks of worth, respect, honor, place in society.

Debility speaks of weakness, illness, lack of strength.

Those two connotations, of relative place in society, and of relative health/illness, are intertwined in their use in astrology.

I want to start with the political meanings of the terms, and examine some of their connotations.

Ordered Universe and Society

The universe of astrology is like an ordered city or society. You could think of our modern model of the solar system, with planets revolving around the Sun while the whole system moves through the galaxy amidst other solar systems, as being like a larger whole including multiple interacting societal units.

We live here on Planet Earth, and in astrology the action and movement on earth is a mirror of the movement of the heavens. The heavens are an orderly and patterned society, and our human society parallels that.

This ties in with one of the core meanings of dignity - to be in one's appropriate place in society. *A planet with dignity is in a place where it recognized and has authority and power*.

Dignity and Responsibility

Having an assigned position in society is not just a matter of receiving benefits. It also means having responsibility within society's collective life. This concept of responsibility is part of the core meaning of dignity.

Each planet has a place to be, a role to play, a job to do, a responsibility it has been given. The different dignities describe different levels of responsibility within the social framework.

Dignity and Testimony

In traditional texts the term testimony is also used for dignity. For example, Jupiter has testimony in Sagittarius as ruler of the sign. To have many testimonies in a sign means to be very dignified.

Testimony is related to the concept of witnessing. In a court case, if you are a witness, you testify to what you have seen. The meaning of witnessing here is also seen in a religious context. For instance, in a traditional Christian church reciting the Creed gives testimony or witness to your faith. It marks you as an insider, an accepted member of the community.

The term testimony is also used to refer to people who will witness, testify or vouch for you. If you enter a new community and someone else who is already a member says, *I know them and I can vouch for them*, you are then accepted based on their word.

We can summarize the core political meaning of the terms dignity and debility here.

*Being in Dignity in general means you are a citizen,
a recognized member of a group, and you belong here,
you have a place. It also includes how it affects you
to have a proper and welcoming place.*

*Being in Debility in general implies being out of place,
being somewhere you don't belong, not fitting in.
It also includes the effect of living out of place.*

Now that we have the political meanings of the terms, we will examine the meanings of dignity and debility as connoting strength and weakness.

Dignity/Debility and Strength/Weakness

In the dictionary definition of debility we saw that the primary metaphor was that of being strengthened or weakened. Even within this overall metaphor, the terms have many different connotations.

The terms apply to strength and weakness. To be dignified is to be strengthened, to be debilitated is to be weakened. The terms also can mean health and illness. To be dignified is to be healthy, to be debilitated is to be unhealthy, wounded, or ill.

Related to that, dignity and debility can mean *ease and lack of ease* - our word disease literally means not being at ease. To be dignified is to be at ease, to be debilitated is to be uneasy.

The concepts also have connotations of *balance and lack of balance*, which plays in with ease and lack of ease. To be dignified is to be balanced and at ease, to be debilitated is to be unbalanced, uneasy.

The terms are also related to *comfort and discomfort*. Where you have dignity you are likely to be comfortable, where you are debilitated you are likely to be uncomfortable.

Fitness and unfitness describe dignity, and the word has multiple connotations. Fitness means healthy, strong, and capable. It also applies to being a good fit for a position or task.

We can sum up the physical meanings of dignity and debility here.

Dignity in general means you are strong, healthy,
balanced, capable, fit.

Debility in general means you are weak, unhealthy,
unbalanced, uncapable, unfit, wearing out.

Now that we have the main meanings laid out, we can tie them together.

How the Meanings Intertwine

The political and physical meanings of dignity and debility play into each other, and reinforce each other.

If you are living in a situation where you are loved and respected and have support you are likely to be fit, balanced and capable. This can mean you are in a phase of the cycle of change where things are growing, established and flourishing.

If you are in a situation where you are not at home, not respected, not supported, you are likely to be stressed, weak, ill and unbalanced. This can mean you are in a phase of the cycle of change where things are shifting, changing form, falling apart or declining. In a positive way, being in a situation where you are not at home can also mean acting as an agent of change.

Given the basic concepts of dignity and debility, we can now consider how they interact with the different dimensions of our lives.

Turf Lords and Time Lords

In modern astrology we tend to think of all the planets being turned on, active and available at the same time. For instance, for a person with Sun in Pisces, you would say that person IS a Pisces. We take it as an identity. This implies that one is always expressing as Sun in Pisces. It implies a one-dimensional self, a single identity, and the Sun sign is a shorthand description of that identity.

Both astrology and human life are more complex and multi-faceted. Thinking of a person as having just a single identity is an over-simplification. It is closer to the truth to describe each of us as having a family or society of different selves that play out in different areas of our lives.

For instance, I have my natal Sun in Pisces, but that part of me is not active at all times, nor is it available and visible in all the different areas of my life. Different people know different parts of me, depending upon the context in which we interact.

When I am in a group of people I don't know well, the people there will likely meet Saturn, who is Lord of my Ascendant. I can come across seeming sullen, withdrawn and defensive - Saturnine. I'm the one who hides in the corner at parties.

When I am comfortable with a small group of close friends, they see my Cancer Moon, or my hyperactive, moody, sometimes manic Mercury in very late Pisces. I'm a different person with close friends than in the larger group.

I am not a single identity, I am more like a family, a society. Welcome to the Republic of Charlie!

> *The roles are defined by context - we play different characters depending on what part of our life we are focusing on at the moment.*

This is not just a psychological division. The different areas of the chart also describe different areas of a person's life. For instance, a person with Moon in Cancer in the seventh house of marriage will likely have a marriage with a Moon in Cancer kind of partner - nurturing, emotional, loyal and so on. The planets are both within us and around us. They describe our psychology and inner lives, and they describe the circumstances and people in our outer lives. Our lives have inner and outer dimensions, and astrology mirrors that.

Traditional astrology emphasizes external and objective events and circumstances, while modern astrology places more emphasis on the internal, psychological dimension. I think our overall practice of astrology is strongest when we include both.

Turf Lords

The chart is a society, the planets are citizens, and the places where they have dignity are their assigned area of responsibility.

Each of the houses in an astrology chart is a different area of life. The planets that have dignity in a house are the Turf Lords, responsible for seeing that the affairs of that house are carried out. The planet's position and condition measures how well or poorly the planet does its job. If you have Aquarius on the Midheaven then the planet Saturn is in charge of implementing your career and reputation. All other planets acting in that house report to Saturn who is the main Turf Lord.

Time Lords

Just as planets divide responsibility in space, they also have different activity through time. Not all planets are equally active at all times. Traditional astrology has different systems for determining when a planet becomes active. These are called Time Lord systems. Some of the meanings of the dignities grew from their use as Time Lord systems, measuring when a given planet would be active.

For example - using secondary progressions, when a planet changes signs, like the progressed Sun moving from Aries into Taurus, the Sun changes its expression suited to the fixed sign Taurus and its rulers. Moving from Aries to Taurus you would experience the Sun slowing down, becoming more deliberate, more grounded, less impulsive, and so on.

In terms of time lords, the Sun has gone from being ruled by Mars to being ruled by Venus. To see how that plays out, you would consider the location of Venus in the chart, its house placement, general condition and aspects. Venus is in charge while the progressed Sun is in Taurus.

Traditional astrology interprets a planet changing signs by examining the placement and condition of the Time Lords in charge of the sign.

Dignity and the meaning of planets in signs

Emphasizing a planet's dignity is a different approach from modern interpretation, which relies on the zodiac signs for primary meaning. A modern astrologer would say that having Sun in Pisces has a group of related meanings. Traditional astrology looks at the Sun's location and condition to interpret that. The condition of the ruling planet gives much of the meaning.

Rulership and the Outer Planets

In terms of the traditional system of astrology, the modern outer planets Uranus, Neptune and Pluto are outsiders. In Dane Rudhyar's metaphor, they are ambassadors from outside of our solar system. There is something distinctly alien about them. They are not regular citizens of our cosmos in the same sense as the traditional seven planets, and they do not have assigned places.

The outer planets do not have rulership or dignity.

This does not say that the modern system of rulership with the outer planets does not produce meaningful symbolism, but that it is not dignity in the traditional sense.

What Dignity and Debility Does Not Mean

I would like to clear up some common misconceptions that cause astrologers to dismiss the use of dignity and debility as harmful and judgmental.

Dignity and debility does not mean good and evil, positive and negative.

To have many dignified planets does not guarantee that your life will be a joy and a success. To have debilitated planets does not mean that your life will be a failure, or that you are doomed to suffering. Being dignified does not mean being a morally good person, and being debilitated does not mean being morally evil.

We will have chart examples showing how dignified planets can be a cause of problems, and debilitated planets can be great sources of strength.

The terms are meant to be evaluative and not judgmental.

Connotations and uses of Dignity and Debility

I think it is clear by now that the concepts of dignity and debility are actually quite rich and complex. Here are some of the connotations of the terms.

- An attitude of good will
- An obligation or duty
- Authority, influence
- Competence, ability to act
- Strength, health
- Recognition, respect, status
- Expressing a quality or type of action - for example, a planet in terms of Mercury will implement things in a Mercury like way
- A measure of attitude - a planet in Libra, where Saturn is exalted, will be treated well by Saturn
- A measure of responsibility - Saturn has responsibility to a planet in Libra.
- Ease and balance
- Belonging, fitting in

Different Categories of Dignities

In Hellenistic astrology there were many different ways of dividing up the heavens and dividing responsibility between the different planets. The main ways of making these divisions of responsibility became what we now call the five different kinds of essential dignity.

First there are the major dignities, and these are familiar to most modern astrologers. There is rulership and its matching debility of detriment, and there is exaltation with its matching debility of fall. In addition there are three other ways of dividing up the heavens that are the minor dignities of triplicity, bound or term, and face.

Each of these dignities has their own particular history and usage, and part of the purpose of this book is to flesh out the meanings of these five dignities and recover some of their nuances.

Along with the essential dignities, there are other conditions called accidental dignities that are also used in evaluating the condition and effectiveness of a planet in a chart. When we have the system put together you will have a multi-level, flexible and powerful way of gauging how planets in a chart pattern will tend to work out.

We will start our study of the dignity system with the two major dignities, rulership and exaltation.

Major Dignities

Rulership and exaltation probably go back to two separate rulership systems, possibly from different countries, that were combined in the Hellenistic synthesis. Some scholars think that the system of rulerships has its origin in Mesopotamia, and the system of exaltation originated in Egypt. Each of these major dignities has a paired opposite point that is a place of debility.

First we will look at rulership and its corresponding debility detriment.

Rulership and the Thema Mundi

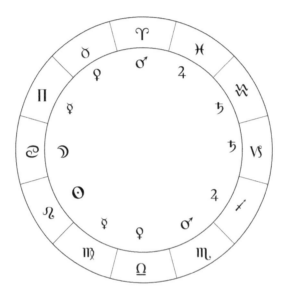

The Latin phrase Thema Mundi means world chart. It is a teaching device showing the signs and planets at the mythical creation of the world. The sign Cancer is rising at the left side of the diagram, and the traditional planets are shown in order based on their relative speed and distance from the earth.

The Thema Mundi diagram shows rulerships. Sun and Moon, the two lights, are on the left side of the diagram in Leo and Cancer. Cancer to Aquarius is the Lunar half of the circle, Leo to Capricorn is the Solar half. The other planets each have two signs, moving out from the lights in the order of their distance from the earth. Mercury takes the two signs adjacent to the lights, Gemini and Virgo, and so on out through to Saturn which takes the signs opposite the lights.

Rulership and Detriment

We will begin with the etymology of the word rulership.

Etymology of Rulership

Rulership is from the Greek **oikodespotes** - oikos meaning family or household, **despotes** meaning ruler or despot- lord of the household. The Arabic **sahib** has a similar meaning.

In early western astrology a zodiac sign is called a Domicile or House. Aries is the Domicile or household of Mars.

The lord and head of a household has authority and control. It implies being among family, being comfortable on your home turf. It means responsibility. The ruler is responsible for seeing that the affairs of that house are properly carried out.

Obligation of Host to Guest

The ruler is host, and has a responsibility to residents and guests in the house. The ruler of the house must treat its guests as well as it can, given its own situation and condition. This concept of obligation of the hosting planet to its guest is a very important part of the meaning of rulership.

Consider this obligation in Richard Wagner's opera *Die Walkure*. In the first scene, the hero Siegmund seeks refuge at the home of Hunding, his mortal enemy. It is a dark and stormy night. Siegmund is wounded and exhausted, and his sword is shattered. He stumbles into the house and throws himself down in front of the hearth and collapses.

In this setting the hearth is a sacred altar. Throwing himself down in front of the fire is a symbolic act, like throwing yourself at the foot of an altar to seek asylum in a church.

When Hunding, lord of the household, arrives home, he finds Siegmund standing in his living room talking to Hunding's wife, Sieglinde. She explains that the man was exhausted and wounded and came here to rest. Hunding's response sums up the obligation of rulership.

Holy is my Hearth, Holy to you be my House.

A little bit later in the scene Hunding discovers that Siegfried is his mortal enemy, the man he had been hunting all day. He tells Siegfried that, for the night, he has asylum in his house and he will honor that. However, when morning comes Siegfried must be prepared to fight.

Hunding has his mortal enemy helpless in front of him in his own house, yet he must still honor his obligation as host to his guest.

The ruler of a sign has the obligation to treat any planet in his sign as his guest. As host, the ruler must act in a helpful way towards its guest to the best of its ability. It is an honor bound obligation.

Rulership in astrology combines the ideas of ownership, of responsibility, of being at home, of authority, and of obligation to care for the affairs of the house and those planets in the house.

Detriment

A planet is in detriment when it occupies the sign opposite to a sign that it rules. For instance, Mars the ruler of Aries is in his detriment in Libra.

Etymology of Detriment

Detriment comes from words meaning to rub down, wear down, wear out, break down. It connotes imbalance, corruption, estrangement, unhealthiness, harm, evil results. Detriment is also related to the word Descension or descending, and to sorrow, pain and distress.

Rulership and detriment are balanced opposites. Rulership is moving up, growing, coming together, and detriment is moving down, aging, coming apart. Detriment is part of a process, the phase which breaks down and assimilates. It is not a matter of rulership being good and detriment being bad. Each is part of a system of balancing opposites moving through time.

There is also a psychological meaning to the term detriment, as shown in this quote from the medieval astrologer Guido Bonatti.

> *"Look to see whether the Lord of some question were in the opposition to its own domicile...Because then the Lord of the matter will be opposed to the purpose for which he asks... nor will it be a matter in which he will delight...it will seem more likely that he does not want it to be perfected." (Consideration #77, 146 Considerations p. 306)*

This implies that a planet in detriment is divided against itself, working on a task where it doesn't really want to succeed. A planet in rulership is at one with itself and its environment, a planet in detriment is at odds with itself and its environment.

Rulership connotes a planet at home, at ease, in control, in balance, calm, able to act in an effective and balanced way that builds things up. A planet in rulership is at home, on its own turf and in control.

A planet in detriment is in an alien environment, not at home, not in control. It will be tense, ill at ease, worried, likely to act in unbalanced or ineffective ways. It will be edgy, nervous and liable to act in a way way that tends to fall apart.

Detriment can have a negative effect. However, detriment can also indicate a planet that learns to function when off-balance and under stress, and those can be strengths.

A planet in detriment can be at odds with itself or its environment, and this can mean being competitive. It can also be a planet doing a needed job in an unsympathetic environment. Detriment can be a planet that has learned to function in a tense, stressful and unfriendly situation. As an outsider, a planet in detriment can be a change agent.

Here are some examples of planets in rulership and detriment.

Mars in Aries (Rulership) - Mars is in control and can act the part of solo warrior strongly and effectively.

Mars in Libra (Detriment) - Mars is out of his element, in a sign where solo, assertive warrior behavior is at odds with a sign ruled by Venus. Consequently he will be ill at ease, tense, nervous, not at home in his environment. Picture Sylvester Stallone playing the lead in Sound of Music.

Mars in detriment could also be a soldier or military man in a situation that doesn't permit him to fight or be aggressive.

Venus in Libra (Rulership) - Venus is at home, balanced, sets the tone and rules, can be relaxed and gracious to others.

Venus in Aries (Detriment) - Venus is in the home of Mars and is influenced to be aggressive, self-focused. Receptivity, graciousness, and balance are not easy to achieve in this setting, it is not a good match. Picture Julie Andrews as Rambo.

In a different setting, Venus in Aries could be a nurse in a war zone, playing a helpful role in a hostile environment.

Here are some charts that illustrate the meaning of rulership and detriment.

Woody Allen

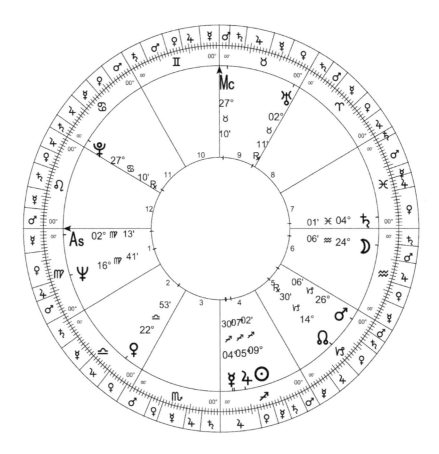

Allen Stewart Konigsberg, December 1, 1935, 10:55 PM, Bronx, New York. Rodden Rating AA. Whole Sign Houses.

The ruler of the Ascendant, Mercury, is in his detriment in Sagittarius. However, Mercury is also conjunct Jupiter, Lord of the household.

I think that Mercury in detriment here represents the bumbling character or stage persona Woody Allen typically plays. The strong supporting influence of Jupiter means that Allen can use the Mercury persona to create his films. This is an example of a detriment used as an asset.

Herman Melville

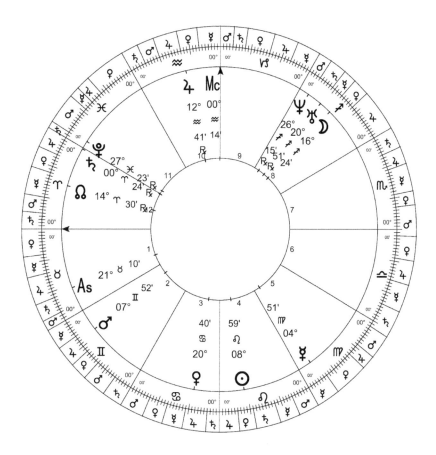

Herman Melville, August 1, 1819, 11:30 PM, New York, New York. Rodden Rating AA. Whole Sign houses.

Mercury is in rulership in Virgo in the fifth house. Mercury is square Mars, and Mars is in Gemini ruled by Mercury. Mercury controls Mars, and is also obligated to see that the affairs of Mars in the second house are taken care of. Melville's best books have a Mercury Mars flavor, chronicling his adventures among South Sea natives in *Typee* or aboard an ill-fated whaling vessel in his masterpiece *Moby Dick*.

Muhammed Ali

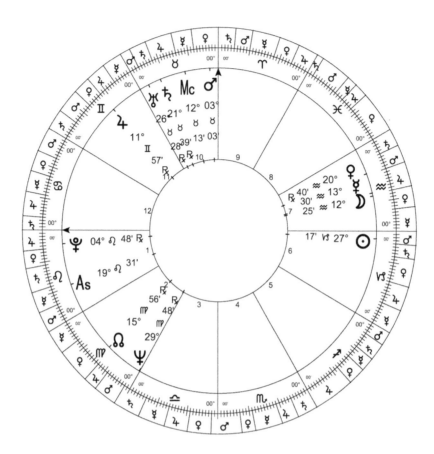

Cassius Marcellus Clay, Jr. January 17, 1942, 6:35 PM, Louisville, Kentucky. Rodden Rating AA. Whole Sign houses.

Mars is in Taurus up in the tenth house, in detriment, and angular, very near the Midheaven. Mars in detriment is often found in competitive sports like boxing, or in the charts of highly competitive people in politics or business.

Note that Mars also rules the ninth house of religion. Ali was imprisoned for draft evasion for refusing to be drafted on religious grounds when he became Muslim. At that period in American history such an act was unthinkable treason. This is Mars in detriment bucking the system in the name of religious freedom.

A Planet Ruling a House

To interpret a house, look at the location and condition of the sign ruler of the house.

When the lord of the house is in its rulership it will be strong, at ease, comfortable, able to take care of its house in a competent manner.

By contrast, if the planetary ruler of a house is in detriment it is off-balanced, ill at ease, and uncomfortable. Despite good intent, the planet is not likely to do a balanced, relaxed job. There will be stresses and challenges in the house affairs.

Charles Obert

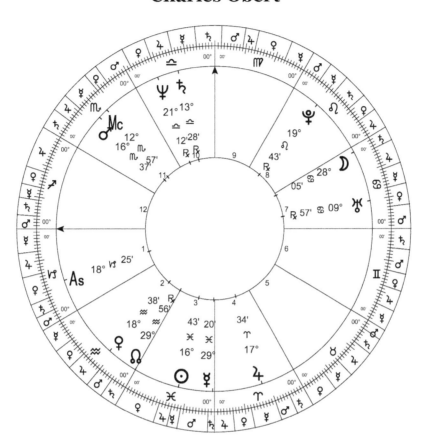

Chart of the author, Charles Obert. March 7, 1952, 3:38 am, Queens, New York. From birth certificate. Whole Sign houses.

In my birth chart the Moon is strong and angular, in its rulership in Cancer in the seventh house. This manifested as a long and stable marriage to a caring and loyal spouse.

By contrast, Mercury is in the third house in Pisces, in detriment and fall. Mercury rules the sixth house of work, and the ninth house of religion. Both areas were unstable and marked by periods in which I felt I was not taken seriously - detriment and fall. Undertakings in those areas had a tendency to fall apart.

Exaltation and Fall

Exaltation probably originated as a separate rulership system. It seems clear that the system of exaltations has its roots in Babylonian tradition.

This diagram shows the seven traditional planets in their exaltation.

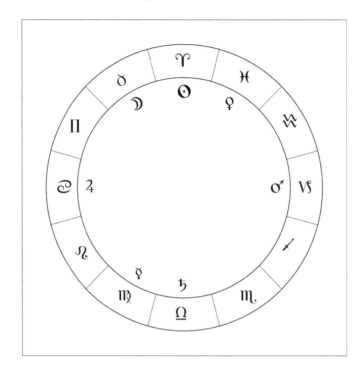

In some early texts exaltation was originally associated with a specific degree, as in the following table.

Sun	19 Aries
Moon	3 Taurus
Mercury	15 Virgo
Venus	27 Pisces
Mars	28 Capricorn
Jupiter	15 Cancer
Saturn	21 Libra

Dorotheus refers to the degree of exaltation, as does Firmicus Maternus. By contrast, Ptolemy in *Tetrabiblos* refers to the exaltation as the sign and does not mention the specific degree. Most later usage applies exaltation to the entire sign, which is how we will be using it here.

Meaning of Exaltation

The dignity of exaltation connotes being honored, esteemed, respected, listened to, raised up.

It can be an honored guest or member of royalty. The word was sometimes translated as **regnum**, meaning kingdom or nobility.

A planet in exaltation receives honor and respect, but it does not have the management or control of rulership. If the ruler of a sign is like the CEO of a company then the exalted ruler would be the owner - respected, honored, even exalted, but not managing the day to day work.

Exaltation can mean being highly valued. Jupiter exalted in the second house of possessions can mean great wealth, or valuable possessions like precious jewelry.

Exaltation can also mean that you are valued in the sense of being listened to and respected.

It can also have a psychological meaning, connoting a person with a high opinion of themselves. The early English astrologer William Lilly links it to arrogance.

Here is a chart example of exaltation that illustrates many of the meanings we have listed.

Charles, Prince of Wales

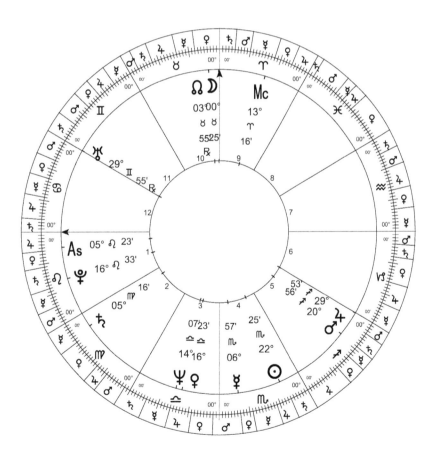

Charles Philip Arthur George Mountbatten-Windsor, November 14, 1948, 9:14 PM, London, England. Rodden Rating A. Whole Sign houses.

This is the chart of Sir Charles Prince of Wales.

Queen Elizabeth is the dominating planet in her son's chart here, represented by the Moon in her exaltation in Taurus in the tenth house, in a role that is more about dignity and show than about power. The Moon is on the North Node, and in traditional astrology the North Node is considered to magnify or strengthen any planets near it. The North Node further magnifies the importance of this exalted Taurus moon. The Moon is in the fixed sign Taurus which signifies endurance over time, and the Queen is very, very long lived.

Meaning of Fall

By contrast with exaltation, a planet in fall is not listened to, not respected, in disgrace. It connotes downfall, slavery, servitude. A planet in fall is not respected, not heard or noticed.

In Greek writings exaltation is sometimes called ***throne*** and fall is called ***prison*** - on the thrones they have royal power, in prison they are abased and oppose their own power.

Fall is the Rodney Dangerfield of the dignities - planets in fall *don't get no respect*. Because planets in fall feel ignored, they can often be driven to act in unbalanced ways to get the attention and respect they want. A planet in fall can try too hard to get attention.

In psychological terms a planet in fall can mean a bad self-image, a low opinion of yourself, or self-loathing. It can be a part of you that you do not value or refuse to listen to.

A friend of mine has the Moon in Scorpio rising in her first house. Talking of emotions, she says that she just refuses to listen to her feelings, she doesn't pay any attention to them because she feels they get her in trouble. That is a good literal example of a planet in fall not being listened to.

Richard Nixon

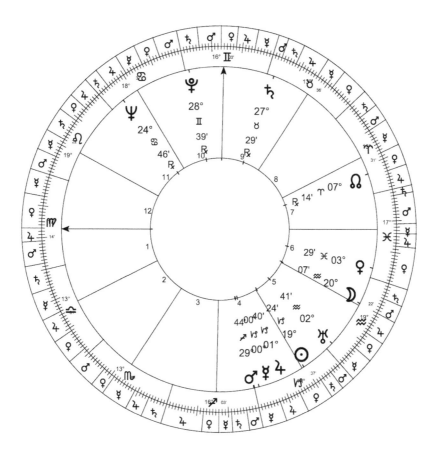

Richard Milhous Nixon, January 9, 1913, Yorba Linda, California. Rodden Rating AA. Placidus Houses.

"I am not a crook." - Richard M. Nixon

Note the conjunction of Mars and Mercury with Jupiter, who is in his fall in Capricorn. These three planets are all opposite Pluto in Gemini up in the tenth house. Power issues...

Planets in fall feel like they get no respect, and so they work very hard to get attention and status. With Jupiter's desire to expand, this can translate into a craving for power, recognition, authority and status. Under stress a planet in fall could be suspicious, paranoid, feeling others are not respecting it.

I think this aptly describes Richard Nixon and his political behavior that led to the Watergate scandal and his threatened impeachment.

Lenny Bruce

Leonard Alfred Schneider, October 13, 1925, 11:24 AM, Mineola, New York. Rodden Rating AA. Whole Sign houses.

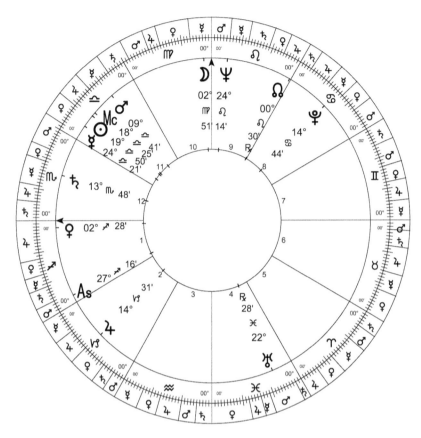

This is an interesting example of a person who built his career on a strong configuration of planets in detriment and fall - the comedian and satirist Lenny Bruce. Bruce was known for his abrasive, politically radical and off-color humor, and he wrote a book titled *How to Talk Dirty and Influence People*. Lenny Bruce strongly influenced the comedian George Carlin.

In this chart we have a T-Square in cardinal signs with Mars in detriment and Sun in fall on either side of the Midheaven, square Jupiter in fall who is opposite Pluto. Planets in fall are ridiculed, not respected, and can take extreme lengths to be noticed. Lenny's Bruce's style of comedy featuring in your face ridicule, obscenity and satire fit planets in detriment and fall.

Ship Lost at Sea

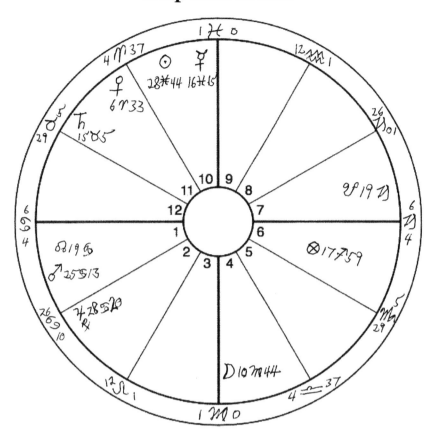

(William Lilly, Christian Astrology Volume Two, p. 165. Regiomontanus houses.)

(Note that I drew this chart by hand to put the planets and house cusps in the exact location that William Lilly used.)

This is a horary chart from William Lilly's *Christian Astrology* about a ship carrying valuable cargo that was damaged and lost at sea. Lilly makes the Moon the main significator of the ship, and shows multiple reasons why it is lost.

The Part of Fortune represents the valuable cargo on the ship. It is in Sagittarius, ruled by a retrograde Jupiter, who is exalted in Cancer in the 2nd house of money, mutually applying to a conjunction with Mars, who is in fall. Fall has to do with not being valued, not being listened to - and in this case, not being heard from. Jupiter is the valuables, Mars is the accident.

Here the meanings of exaltation and fall colliding can be taken literally. A load of highly valued cargo is never heard from again.

Using Major Dignities in Chart Interpretation

You can learn a lot about a chart just by paying attention to those planets which have a major dignity or debility. This is an excellent place to start in chart analysis.

Scan the chart for the major dignities and debilities of rulership and detriment, exaltation and fall. Planets which are strongly dignified or debilitated are likely to figure prominently in the person's life.

I hope it is clear by now that debility is not always negative, and a planet in debility is not necessarily a liability. It can end up being an asset, but it sometimes takes its own way of being worked.

This is particularly important with natal charts, where the person has a lifetime to learn how to work with it. With a planet in debility there may be a period where one needs to experience the down side of the planet before mastering the up side. This is a process of acclimation that goes on over time. Planets get used to their environment and learn how to function.

Planets in debility are also strongly influenced by the location and condition of their rulers. We saw that in Woody Allen's chart, where Mercury in debility is greatly strengthened by being conjunct its ruler Jupiter.

A Study of Detriment and Fall

I want to illustrate how a debilitated planet can exhibit a range of characteristics that are both positive and negative. This is a detailed look at a debilitated planet I know from a lifetime of experience - Mercury in Pisces in my own natal chart. Mercury in Pisces is in both detriment and fall, so it is doubly debilitated.

This does not mean I am not intelligent or that I cannot communicate verbally, since you are reading this book that I wrote. This discredits the notion that a planet in detriment and fall cannot express positively.

However, I want to consider the meanings of those two terms here, detriment and fall, and see how they have played out in my life.

A planet in detriment is said to be out of control, scattered, not in its element. Projects started tend to fall apart and come to nothing. There is a lack of ease, a lack of comfort, and the feeling of not being at home.

A planet in fall is not respected, not heard or listened to and is accorded little honor.

Can I see evidence of these problems with detriment and fall? Very much so, and I wish I had been conscious of them much earlier in my life. It would have saved me a lot of grief.

About detriment, I can't count the number of book projects I have started writing and not finished. When I read, my attention often jumps all over the place, and I will often pick up one book, read a couple of pages, then put it down and jump over to another.

Another characteristic of Mercury in detriment is playing loose with the truth, lying and being deceitful. When I was younger you could describe me as an oblivious liar. I thought of myself as basically truthful, but I didn't mind stretching things a bit - maybe more than a bit - okay, a lot – to make myself look good. I got myself in serious trouble that way.

About fall, I have often had the experience of feeling like I was being ignored, not taken seriously and not listened to. Have you ever had the experience in a meeting of making a suggestion and having it blown off, then having someone else make exactly the same suggestion a little later and have it be welcomed? I've experienced that a lot.

Internally I have always felt that the way I think was kind of odd, out of sync with the world around me, so I felt misunderstood and not listened to. After one too many funny looks when I spoke my mind I learned to keep my mouth shut. I also learned how to play the game of fitting in with the world around me.

Have I made this difficulty work in my favor? Yes, I think so. Precisely because issues with Mercury were a problem, a sore spot, I spent a great deal of time and effort studying and working on all aspects of the mind and communication, both verbal and non-verbal. Over the years I think this has given me the ability to articulate what I am thinking and feeling quite clearly, and also to listen carefully to how others communicate, to really hear what they are saying.

I try to speak only truthfully, but I am often aware of the desire or tendency to clean things up a bit to look better. Do I think I am completely truthful? No, but I think the "stretches" get less frequent and less stretchy. However, that tendency to want to lie is part of who I am. It's not going anywhere, and I have to learn to be conscious of it and to deal with it, particularly because part of its effect is to buy my own lies, to lie to myself.

Do I feel that I look at the world differently than most people around me? Yes, I do, and after much work I have gotten pretty good at communicating what I am thinking in a way that is often well received precisely because it is different, a bit odd, a bit out of the norm.

That was a long hard road of learning, especially when I was younger and wasn't very aware of what was going on.

In interpreting dignities and debilities, I think that the most useful approach is to seek a place of balance. It is good to face problems and challenges and not to gloss over them, and it is also good to consider ways in which those problems and challenges can be dealt with, used, and perhaps turned into assets.

Such an approach allows for the great power of human free will and choice, while also recognizing that our choice is limited, and that sometimes we are faced with situations that really are outside of our responsibility and control. In such a case, the best that we can do is to consider strategies for handling the situation.

The concepts of dignity and debility, rulership and exaltation, detriment and fall, are not judgmental terms, they are descriptive terms. Talking about problems or difficulties is not a put-down and does not mean a person is destined to be second rate. It does mean that there is work to do, and an increase in awareness is helpful and necessary to deal with the problems.

Now I think we are ready to move on to an examination of the minor dignities.

Minor Dignities

The combined system of major and minor dignities are part of the Hellenistic synthesis that is the root of our astrology. To really understand them, I think it is important to realize that this combination of dignities did not begin as a combined and integrated system. Rather, it is likely that each of the dignities were used as separate rulerships before they were combined as a system. Each has their own history, their own particular meaning and usage. All five of the dignities are in early Hellenistic texts, but they are not consistently or equally used.

All of the dignities have connotations of strength, responsibility, recognition, and ability to act well. The minor dignities represent ways that different levels of responsibility were assigned to the planets.

The two major dignities, rulership and exaltation, both give a single planet to an entire sign. You do not see that single sign, single planet connection with any of the minor dignities.

The minor dignity of triplicity assigns multiple planets to a single sign according to element, so that we have a group of planets assigned jurisdiction to a group of signs.

By contrast, the minor dignities of bound (or term) and face are different ways of dividing up the chart into smaller divisions within signs, other than by sign, and assigning rulerships to those sections. There are also other ways of dividing up the chart, like the twelfth parts or ninth parts, that were important, but did not become part of the essential dignity system. Some of these alternate systems are still used today, and even though they are not part of the formal dignity system they do have some of the same characteristics of assigning a planet jurisdiction to a portion of a sign.

Unlike the major dignities, these minor dignities do not have a corresponding debility.

Sect

The dignity of triplicity is related to the more basic division of sect, so we need to examine that first. The concept of sect was originally very important, even central in Hellenistic astrology.

Sect is built on the most basic two-fold division of astrology into day and night, diurnal and nocturnal. The planets are divided into two groups by sect along these lines, as shown in the following table and diagram.

	Light	Benefic	Malefic
Diurnal	Sun	Jupiter	Saturn
Nocturnal	Moon	Venus	Mars

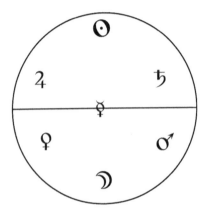

Each of the two sects contains three planets - one light, one benefic (beneficial and easy), and one malefic (harmful, challenging, difficult).

The sect of Mercury can vary, and it is determined by its position relative to the Sun. Mercury rising before the Sun is diurnal, rising after the Sun is nocturnal.

Sect is an overall chart dignity that sets planets as in or out of sect depending on whether or not they agree with the sect of the chart. Think of the division of sect as being like a pair of teams or political parties. It is primarily a political term, and has to do with team membership and support. It also connotes family or tribe, being an insider of a group and having group support.

Sect in later traditional astrology

In later traditional astrology there was a further development of the concept of sect that included looking at whether a planet was above or below the horizon, and whether its sect matched the sect of the sign it was in.

I want to make clear that I am using sect in the earlier, simpler meaning of the term, referring only to whether a chart is day or night, and whether a given

planet is in or out of the overall sect of the chart.

Effect of Sect

A Planet is more at home and effective in a chart matching its sect. A Planet is less effective or more disruptive in a chart not matching its sect. A benefic in its own sect is more helpful than if it is out of sect. A malefic in its own sect is less harmful than when out of sect.

To get an idea of how much difference the sect of a planet makes in Hellenistic astrology, consider the following quote from the fourth century writer Firmicus Maternus.

> *Venus posited in the 4th house from the Ascendant by day...will make a very great loss of inheritance and continual bereavements, and it will make such persons as can only get things with difficulty...*

> *But if it was found in this house by night, with the passage of time it will make praises, friends of great men, and those full of charm and handsome. (Mathesis 132-133)*

The difference is not subtle; it is quite extreme.

Using Sect in Delineation

You can find the sect of the chart by looking at the location of the Sun - day or night, diurnal or nocturnal, above or below the Ascendant/Descendant line.

One you have determined the sect of the chart, locate the benefics and malefics in and out of sect, and look at houses they occupy and those that they rule. Other things being equal, the benefic matching the chart sect will be a main source of benefit, and the malefic not matching the chart sect will be a main source of misfortune and difficulty.

Note that if the Sun is very near either the Ascendant or Descendant, meaning near sunrise or sunset, this can be a judgment call as to whether the chart is considered diurnal or nocturnal. When the Sun is just below the horizon the sky is still quite light, so it can sometimes work to judge that a diurnal chart even with the Sun being just below the horizon.

A good way to test a borderline chart is to ask the subject which of the two malefics seems to be the greater source of difficulty. It is often easier and more vivid to identify problem areas than those areas that are going well. Problem areas usually get more conscious attention and focus.

Here are some simple examples of how the out of sect malefic can determine major problem areas in a person's life.

Charles Obert

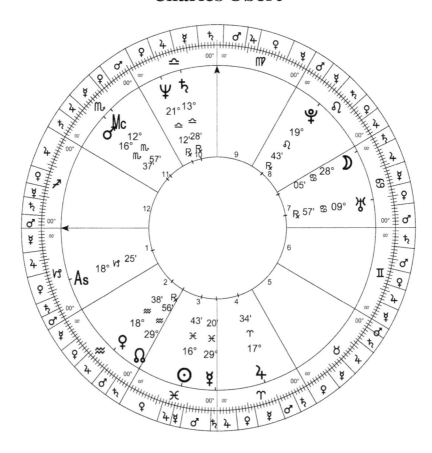

Charles Obert, the author - see previous example for data.

My natal chart is a night chart - I was born at 3:38 am - with the Sun below the horizon in Pisces in the third house.

Saturn is the malefic out of sect, ruling the first and second houses. Poor self image and financial problems have been ongoing issues in my life. Jupiter, being out of sect, will not be as helpful as if it were in a day chart, and it is in opposition to Saturn. Jupiter transits for me are weak, problematic or mixed in effect.

Venus, the benefic matching the sect of the chart, will likely be a major source of benefit and good fortune, according to its placement and general condition. Note that Venus is in a trine relationship with Saturn, and that each of these planets is in a sign where the other planet is dignified. This moderates the worst effect of the out of sect Saturn and helps it end up working to my advantage - not fun, not easy, but with worthwhile results. Saturn in turn adds a difficult edge to my good fortune - my worst misfortune and my best fortune are intertwined.

Mars, the malefic matching the sect of the chart, is still a malefic, but the problems and challenges that Mars represents mostly end up working to my advantage - Mars is on the team in power in the chart.

Client Chart

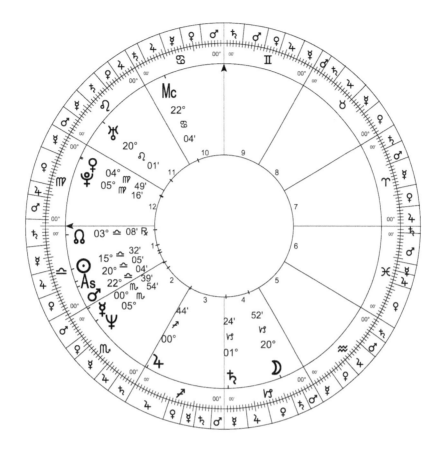

This chart is from a client, data withheld. Chart is from birth certificate. Whole Sign houses.

This example is a day chart. The Ascendant is at 20 Libra, and the Sun is above the horizon at 15 Libra.

Mars is the malefic out of sect, ruling houses two and seven. Primary relationships and financial matters will likely be ongoing problem areas. Venus is the out of sect benefic, and in this chart she is hampered by being in her fall in the twelfth house so that she will be of limited benefit.

Jupiter, the benefic of the day, and Saturn, the malefic of the day, will likely be sources of benefit to the person, especially since they are both dignified by rulership in this chart.

Now that we have the basic meaning of sect we can examine the minor dignity that is based on sect, that of triplicity.

Triplicity

The term triplicity or trigon refers to the signs grouped in threes according to the four elements, fire, water, air and earth. The two diurnal elements, fire and air, are given diurnal triplicity rulers, and the two nocturnal elements, water and earth, are given nocturnal triplicity rulers.

Note that the triplicity rulers of a planet or house are determined only by the element of the sign it is in, and is not determined by the overall sect of the chart.

These two quotes from Dorotheus, an early Greek writer whose work was enormously influential in the western tradition, gives an idea of how very important sect is in Hellenistic astrology.

> *"And I inform you that every thing which is decided and indicated comes to be from the lords of the triplicities." (ch. 1.1, 8.)*

> *"Every planetary fortune, if it was in its own house, or in its own triplicity or its elevation, then what it indicates of the good will be powerful and increasing."(ch. 1.6, 2.)* Elevation is an another translation of exaltation.

Note that here, in this very early material, triplicity is considered equal to the two major dignities, rulership and exaltation. In fact, in Dorotheus the triplicity rulers are often given the strongest emphasis.

Versions of Triplicity Rulers

There are two main systems of assigning triplicity rulers in the Hellenistic tradition. The version we know as the Dorothean triplicities is most likely the earliest. This version appears in Vettius Valens and in Dorotheus, two of the earliest practical texts of Hellenistic astrology still extant. This is the version that we will be using in this text.

Element	Day	Night	Partner
Fire	Sun	Jupiter	Saturn
Air	Saturn	Mercury	Jupiter
Water	Venus	Mars	Moon
Earth	Venus	Moon	Mars

Paul of Alexandria, another early author, uses the same attributions for day and night, but omits mention of the third partner planet. The following quote from Paul is typical of how he describes the triplicities as part of defining the signs.

"The beginning of the zodiacal circle is Aries...vernal domicile of Mars, exaltation of the Sun around 19 degrees, fall of Saturn around 20 degrees; triplicity by day of the Sun, and by night of Jupiter."(p.2)

Note that, in Paul as in Dorotheus, triplicity was considered an important enough dignity to be listed with domicile rulership and exaltation. Also note that only one ruler is used by day or night, and the third participating planet is not mentioned.

The following quote is from Al-Biruni, an Arabic author from the tenth century whose work is a compilation of earlier traditions. This gives a good idea of how the three triplicity rulers were used.

"Each triplicity has a lord by day and another by night, also a third which shares this responsibility by day and night."

"Thus the fiery triplicity has as Lord the Sun by day and Jupiter by night, while Saturn is a partner both by day and night."(p.47.)

In these quotes we see that Al-Biruni's triplicities are the same as Dorotheus, and he uses them in pairs, the ruler matching the sect of the chart plus the partner planet.

Ptolemy's Triplicity System

There is an alternate version of the triplicity rulers, attributed to Ptolemy, and used in his widely influential text, *Tetrabiblos*. Ptolemy gives each element one triplicity ruler by day, and one by night. He does not mention the third partner planet.

Element	Day	Night
Fire	Sun	Jupiter
Air	Saturn	Mercury
Water	Mars	Mars
Earth	Venus	Moon

Note that this system differs from the Dorothean, by giving Water to the planet Mars for both day and night.

Ptolemy's work was very highly regarded, and this single ruler triplicity system became the norm in much of the Western astrology tradition, and was adopted by William Lilly. This is the most widely used triplicity system used in modern horary practice that traces its lineage to Lilly.

Which Planets to Use?

Along with there being two different systems of triplicity rulers, there is an inconsistency in how the triplicity rulers are used in the older Dorothean system. Some authors use just one of the rulers, some two, some all three. There is also an inconsistency in how they were used in pairs - sometimes the diurnal and nocturnal rulers were used and the participating planet was ignored, sometimes the planet in sect was paired with the participating planet.

I use all three triplicity rulers as a group.

The three triplicity rulers are member of the ruling party or group in control, so it makes most sense to me to use all three of them, and to view them as working together.

Triplicity Lords of the Sect Light

One way to evaluate the overall condition of a chart is to look at the three triplicity lords of the light that matches the sect of a chart - the Sun for a day chart, the Moon for a night chart. These three triplicity lords were evaluated to judge the general good or bad fortune a person would experience. This system was widely used by Dorotheus in the Hellenistic era. It is also featured in the Arabic text, *The Judgment of Nativities*, by Abu'Ali, and in Bonatti's medieval compilation.

A similar procedure of evaluating the three triplicity lords was also applied to houses and specific topics. For instance, to see how a person will do financially, you would look at the triplicity lords of the sign on the cusp of the 2nd house.

The following two examples are from Dorotheus.

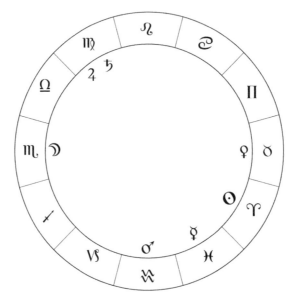

"Another native: his Ascendant, rising up from the earth, was Scorpio, and the native was nocturnal, and the positions of the planets were according to what is in the image. And the lord of the triplicities of the Moon is Mars, then Venus, then the Moon. Since the three of

them were in a stake (angular), that man was powerful in nobility, powerful in leadership until crowns of gold and silver were put on him, and he was praised." (ch 1, 26, 9-11)

Here is a contrasting chart example from Dorotheus.

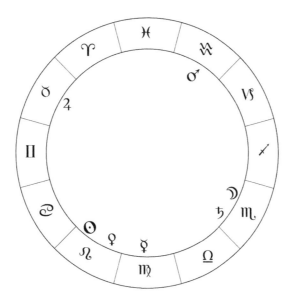

"The native was nocturnal, and I found the most worthy of the planets in the matter of his good fortune to be Mars and Venus, because they are the lords of the triplicities of the sign in which the Moon was, and they were both in a falling place (cadent), so that man was in need, poor, not finding his daily bread, having toil." (ch.1.26, 3.)

In both of these examples Dorotheus evaluates the triplicity rulers as strong if they in an angular house, and weak if they are in a cadent house. No other conditions are weighed. These examples suggest that triplicity was used as a primary way of judging a chart before the current system of essential dignities was put together. It also suggests that angularity was the primary method of judging the strength or weakness of a planet.

Following Dorotheus, triplicity was widely used by Persian and Arabic astrologers. The examples that I quoted above from Dorotheus also appear in Abu'Ali's Judgment *of Nativities,* an Arabic astrology textbook from the early ninth century.

Interpreting Triplicity

 The meaning of triplicity grows out of its connection with sect, in the sense of dividing the planets up into tribes, families or teams.

A planet in its triplicity is in harmony with the group or family in which it functions. Planets in triplicity do not "rule the house", but they have a place and authority to function in a group. Triplicity rulership is where you have friends, you have support. Since triplicity is a group dignity it makes most sense to use all three planets as a group, without being concerned with their relative ranking.

As we saw in the examples from Dorotheus, the triplicity rulers of the sect light can be considered as contributing to general good or ill fortune, of general support or lack thereof. A triplicity ruler in good shape can increase a person's good fortune, and a ruler in bad shape can decrease that fortune.

Triplicity and elemental balance align, since the triplicity lords are determined based on element. A planet that has dignity by triplicity is in its element.

The best case for a planet is to be both in triplicity by element and also match the sect of the chart. Sect and triplicity measure different levels of general group belonging, with sect being broader (referring to the entire chart) and triplicity more specific (referring to the sign and element).

William Burroughs

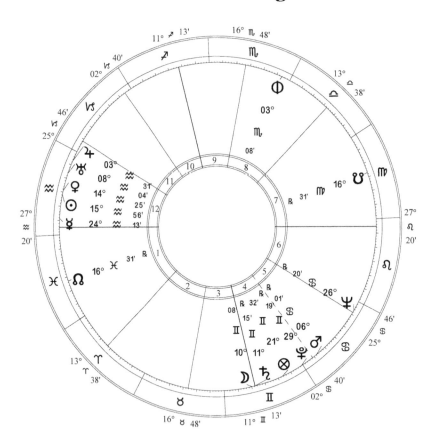

William Seward Burroughs, February 5, 1914, 7:40 AM, St Louis, Missouri. Rodden Rating AA. Placidus Houses.

Consider the renegade Mars, in the fifth house in Cancer.

All other planets except Neptune are in the two air signs Aquarius and Gemini. Mars is the sole traditional planet in a water sign. Mars is also averse all the other signs, meaning it makes no aspects to the other planets. This isolates Mars, leaving it out of touch.

Mars is in its fall, but it does have dignity by triplicity and bound, so it has some strength and competence, but with a lack of authority and respect. Mars is also out of sect in this day chart.

The other members of his triplicity family, Venus and the Moon, are both in very bad shape, with Venus being combust (burnt up by being near the Sun), and Moon applying to a tight conjunction with Saturn. Mars lacks any effective support from its triplicity family.

Looking at the other planets, the sect light is the Sun since this is a day chart, and the triplicity lords of the Sun are Saturn, Mercury and Jupiter. Two of those planets, Mercury and Saturn, dominate the chart, each being in the sign that the other rules, and each of them is conjunct an angle.

Mercury and Saturn dominate his conscious personality, and Mars is a strong and violent part of him outside of conscious awareness and control. That Mars found tragic expression in September 1951, when Burroughs shot and killed his wife Joan Vollmer during a drunken William Tell stunt at a party. This was the defining act of his life that haunted and drove him in the desperate dark search depicted in his writing.

The following quote from Burroughs is from the introduction to the early novel *Queer*.

*"I am forced to the appalling conclusion that I would have never become a writer but for Joan's death ... [S]o **the death of Joan brought me into contact with the invader, the Ugly Spirit**, and maneuvered me into a lifelong struggle, in which I had no choice except to write my way out". (Burroughs, Queer, published 1985, p.xxii)*

Mars is the Ugly Spirit, the invader, a dark demon of his unconscious mind. His conscious mind dominated by Saturn and Mercury had to wrestle that demon in his writing. In modern astrology terms, his renegade Mars is in the fifth house that is associated with creativity like fiction.

This chart shows how triplicity membership can give a feeling for the overall fit and support of a planet within the chart as a whole.

Warren Buffet

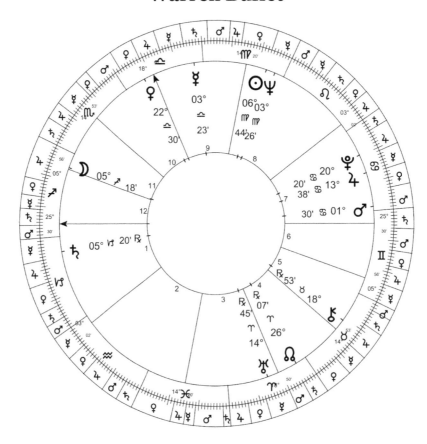

Warren Edward Buffet, August 30, 1930, Omaha, Nebraska. Rodden Rating A. Placidus houses.

Warren Buffet is well known as one of the wealthiest men in the world, so we should expect to see indications of general good fortune.

This is a day chart, and the sect light, the Sun, is in Virgo. The three triplicity lords of Virgo are Venus, then the Moon, then Mars. Two of the three of them, Venus and Mars, are the two most angular planets in the chart, and Venus is strengthened by being in her rulership in Libra and in her own bounds. Angularity is the main marker of strength that Dorotheus uses, and that applies well to this chart.

Triplicity Lords as Successive Phases

Another early use of the triplicity lords was to divide up a person's life into periods, and use each of the triplicity lords to govern that part of a person's life.

There are different versions in the tradition concerning how this dividing into phases was done. The earliest system used only the first two triplicity lords, and the partner was sometimes viewed as supporting both, and sometimes omitted. Later tradition used a sequence of three triplicity lords.

This division into phases was most commonly done with the triplicity lords of the sect light, but it was also applied to specific topics. So, for instance, if the question were about finances, the triplicity lords of the sign of the second house would be used to look at financial condition throughout life. The better condition the three of them were in generally, the better would be the person's overall financial condition. Then the lords were looked at in turn as ruling over three phases of a person's life.

In the following example the three triplicity lords in succession have parallels in the periods of good and bad fortune in Henry Miller's life.

Henry Miller

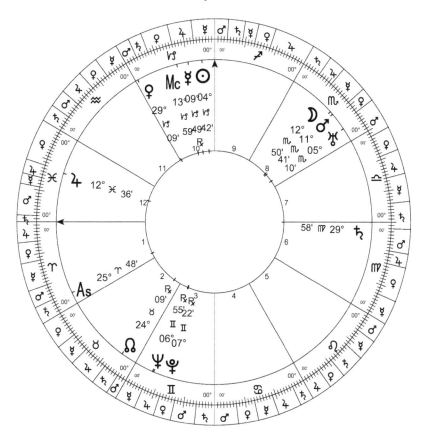

Henry Valentine Miller, December 26, 1891, 12:30 PM, Manhattan, New York. Rodden Rating A. Whole Sign houses.

This is a day chart, with the Sun up near the Midheaven in the tenth house. The triplicity lords of Sun Capricorn, an earth sign, are Venus, then the Moon, then Mars. Venus is in the tenth house and angular, and has dignity by triplicity. It is in reasonable shape, and the early years of Miller's life were reasonably secure.

For the second period, the Moon is in detriment and conjunct Mars, in very poor shape. This middle period of Miller's life was his most creative, but it was also very difficult financially - he had long stretches where he was homeless and broke, living from meal to meal, sometimes in fear of starvation.

Mars, the third triplicity lord, is the strongest of the three, in its rulership and triplicity, although it is hampered by being in the eighth house. In the latter part of his life Miller did get both recognition and financial success, and was quite well off when he died. It is interesting that Mars is secluded in the 8th house, and Miller did seclude himself somewhat in his last years.

Napoleon Bonaparte

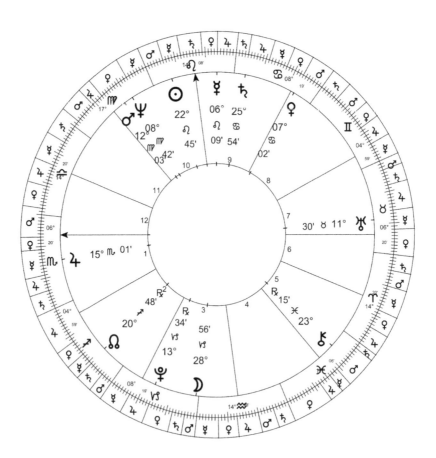

Napoleone di Buonaparte, August 15, 1769, Ajaccio, France. Rodden Rating A. Placidus houses.

This is a day chart, and the triplicity lords of the Sun are the Sun itself, Jupiter, and Saturn. The Sun is gloriously strong and prominent, in its own sign and angular near the Midheaven. The second triplicity lord, Jupiter, is also angular near the Ascendant, so two of the three triplicity lords are strong and angular.

The third triplicity lord, Saturn, is cadent in the ninth house, and in its fall in Cancer.

In this case the two strong triplicity lords followed by a weak and cadent third lord parallels Napoleon's fortunate ascent to power, followed at the end of his life by his defeat, and his death in exile.

There does not seem to be a clear guide in early astrology texts as to how long these three phases of a person's life would be in years. I get the sense it is mostly used by taking the person's life span and dividing it into three roughly even parts - but this depends on knowing the date of death and how long a person lived.

While I do not find this timing technique of sequencing the triplicity lords to be consistently useful, I do find is it worth checking the three triplicity lords of the sect light and their general condition without considering sequence. Triplicity rulers contribute to the level of general fortune, support and increase within a given topic.

Bounds or Terms

Bound or term are two names for the same dignity. Each of the words has useful connotations in English, and I will use both.

Bound or term is from the Greek word **horia,** meaning boundary. The Latin equivalent is **termini**. The word refers to a small enclosed area. It is a specific defined area like a garden patch.

Keep these two concepts of specificity and implementation in mind. A bound ruler is in charge of executing things in just that one area like a low level manager or supervisor. This is the planet that sees to how things get done.

The bound rulership system uses only the five planets other than the Sun and Moon.

Bounds are Time Related

In its original usage, the bounds or terms are related to a measure or division of time, and it appears that they were originally used to calculate length of life.

This quote from Paul of Alexandria is an example of referring to the bounds or terms in a time context.

> *"For by means of these same (terms) the wise men of the Egyptians judged the matter of the Ruler of the Nativity from which also the matter of the length of life is determined.*
>
> *"...the number of the terms was completed by the summation of the terms, of which each of the stars was allotted a number in each sign - the summation giving the full years of the life." (p.9)*

Greater Years of the Planets

When measuring the length of life, each of the planets are given a Greater, Middle, and Lesser number of years that the planet would contribute to lifespan. The total degrees ruled by a planet in all of its bounds adds up to its Greater Years.

The total years of the five planets other than the Sun and Moon add up to 360, the number of degrees in the zodiac circle, and each of the planets rules over a total number of degrees equal to its greater years.

The following table shows the five planets, other than the Sun and Moon, and their planetary years.

Planet	Years
Mercury	76
Venus	82
Mars	66
Jupiter	79
Saturn	57
Total	**360**

Versions of the Bounds

As with the triplicity rulers, there are two major versions of dividing the signs into bounds. The earliest version is known as the Egyptian bounds, and this is the version found in Dorotheus, in Vettius Valens, and in Paul of Alexandria. Since it is the earliest version, we will use the Dorothean bounds in this book.

The Bounds According to Dorotheus

♈	0	♃	6	♀	12	☿	20	♂	25	♄
♉	0	♀	8	☿	14	♃	22	♄	27	♂
♊	0	☿	6	♃	12	♀	17	♂	24	♄
♋	0	♂	7	♀	13	☿	18	♃	26	♄
♌	0	♃	6	♀	11	♄	18	☿	24	♂
♍	0	☿	7	♀	17	♃	21	♂	28	♄
♎	0	♄	6	☿	14	♃	21	♀	28	♂
♏	0	♂	7	♀	11	☿	19	♃	24	♄
♐	0	♃	12	♀	17	☿	21	♄	26	♂
♑	0	☿	7	♃	14	♀	22	♄	26	♂
♒	0	☿	7	♀	13	♃	20	♂	25	♄
♓	0	♀	12	♃	16	☿	19	♂	28	♄

Also like the triplicity rulers, there is an alternate version of the division into bounds that originated with Ptolemy. Ptolemy said that the Egyptian version of the bounds did not make sense, and he claimed to have found a secret old manuscript that showed an alternate version he viewed as correct.

Bounds According to Ptolemy

♈	0	♃	6	♀	14	☿	21	♂	26	♄
♉	0	♀	8	☿	15	♃	22	♄	26	♂
♊	0	☿	7	♃	14	♀	21	♄	25	♂
♋	0	♂	6	♃	13	☿	20	♀	27	♄
♌	0	♄	6	☿	13	♀	19	♃	25	♂
♍	0	☿	7	♀	13	♃	18	♄	24	♂
♎	0	♄	6	♀	11	♃	19	☿	24	♂
♏	0	♂	6	♃	14	♀	21	☿	27	♄
♐	0	♃	8	♀	14	☿	19	♄	25	♂
♑	0	♀	6	☿	12	♃	19	♂	25	♄
♒	0	♄	6	☿	12	♀	20	♃	25	♂
♓	0	♀	8	♃	14	☿	20	♂	26	♄

If you look at the two different versions they have the same basic layout, but there are differences in details. For instance, if you look at the bounds for Aries and Taurus, the planet assignments are in the same order, but the number of degrees for each bound is different. If you examine the bounds for Cancer in the two systems, the planets are assigned in a different order.

Reasons for specific division unknown

While the logic for the exact division of the bounds has been lost, there are some general patterns to the division. The total number of degrees adds up to the greater planetary years for predicting length of life. Most of the bounds start with a benefic, and all of the bounds end with a malefic, Saturn or Mars, usually the one that would be most harmful to the sign it is in. This is a main reason why late degrees of a sign are considered to be unfortunate. I think this is related to the malefic's general purpose of breaking down forms at end of a cycle.

We will now look at quotes from some early authors to get an idea of how the bounds were described and used.

Here is an example of description of the bounds from The Hellenistic writer Vettius Valens.

"The first 6° of Aries belong to Jupiter: temperate, robust, prolific, beneficent.

The next 6° belong to Venus: cheerful, clever, radiant, even, pure and handsome.

The following 8° fall under the ambiguous influence of Mercury: changeable, clever, idle, windy, stormy, full of thunder and lightning.

The next 5° belong to Mars: baneful, fiery, unsteady, characteristic of rash, wicked men.

The next 5° belong to Saturn: cold, barren, malicious, injured.

This next quote is from Rhetorius, a Greek writer on astrology from the late Hellenistic era.

"Now, whenever one of the stars (planets) is found in the domicile of a benefic and in the bounds of a benefic having significance for the nativity, it benefits the fortune;

And if it is found in the domicile of a benefic but in the bounds of a malefic, it reduces the good of the fortune;

But if it chances to be in the domicile of a malefic and in the bounds of a malefic, it hurts and darkens his luck.

Now the force of the bounds alters the astrological influences of the stars (planets)..."
(p.13)

Note that in these quotes, the bound rulers are used in combination with the domicile rulers, with the bound ruler modifying the general effect of the domicile ruler for good or ill. The bound ruler is responsible for implementing the agenda of the domicile ruler, so the condition of the bound ruler modifies the quality.

Meaning of Bound in Interpretation

The bound ruler is the planet responsible for implementation of the given matter. Bound shows competency to act in that area. This means that the bound ruler is in charge of how things are done, and does them "on their own terms", with their own set of rules.

This is bound meaning boundary or specific area, and also term meaning the terms or rules which set the boundaries for how things are done. The domicile ruler needs to work through the bound ruler to implement its agenda, as indicated in the quote from Rhetorius that we looked at.

Maya Angelou

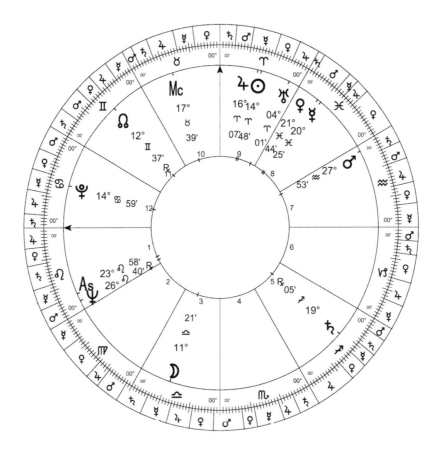

Marguerite Ann Johnson, April 4, 1928, 2:10 PM, St Louis, Missouri. Rodden Rating AA. Whole Sign houses.

This is a good example of predominance of a single planet in this dignity. Note the tight cardinal T-square, with Sun, Jupiter, Moon and Pluto. All four planets and the Ascendant are all in the bounds of Mercury. Bounds concern how things are implemented, and Maya Angelou is a writer, a poet.

Of all the minor dignities, I think that term or bound is the strongest and most under-rated in terms of significance. With its role as the implementation planet, the planet that the ruler has to act through in order to accomplish its agenda, I think paying attention to the bounds can add useful detail.

When I interpret a chart, I always look at the bound rulers of the Ascendant and the Midheaven. Being the main angles, they represent how the person acts in the world.

I also look at the bounds in general for all of the planets to see if there is any predominance of one or two planets. If three or more of the bounds are ruled by a single planet, this planet will likely have a strong influence on how the person acts. The person turns to this bound ruler when it is time to get things done. We saw this in the chart of Maya Angelou.

Here are some examples of using the dignity of term or bound in chart interpretation.

Thomas Merton

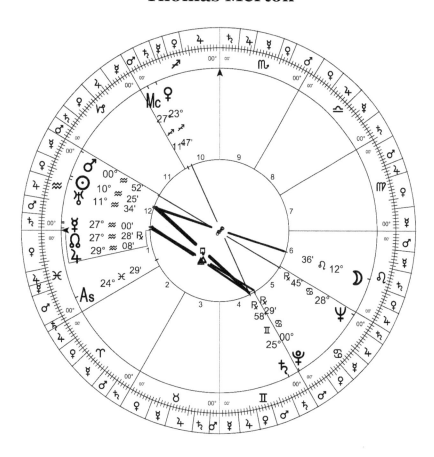

Thomas Merton, January 31, 1915, 9 AM, Prades/Pyrenees Orientales, France. Rodden Rating AA. Whole Sign houses.

The dominance of Saturn in this chart is obvious, with that massive 5 planet stellium in Aquarius in the 12th house of self-renunciation, the path of the strict Trappist monk. Saturn itself is in Gemini in tight trine to Mercury in Aquarius, and the two planets are in mutual reception, with Saturn ruled by Mercury and Mercury ruled by Saturn.

This is further emphasized when you look at the bounds. Starting at the top of the chart, Venus, Mercury, the North Node, Jupiter, Saturn itself, Neptune and the Moon are all in the bounds of Saturn - that is five of the nine traditional planets plus Neptune and the Node. With that strong a predominance, Merton would tend to implement and act in terms of Saturn.

Pope Benedict XVI

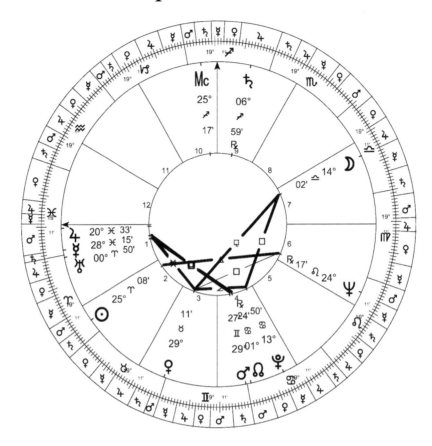

Joseph Alois Ratzinger, April 16, 1927, Marktl, Germany. Rodden Rating AA. Placidus houses.

The most obvious configuration in Pope Benedict's chart is the planet Jupiter in rulership, the rising planet, tightly conjunct the Ascendant in Pisces, ruling the Sagittarius Midheaven - Jupiter, natural significator of the Church. This man was born to be Pope.

Here I want to concentrate on the terms, which are shown on the outer ring of this wheel.

Three of the 7 inner planets, the Sun, Mercury, and Mars, plus the Midheaven, are all in the terms of Saturn. Two of the remaining planets, Venus and Jupiter, are in the terms of Mars, while Mars himself is in the terms of Saturn. The remaining two planets, Moon and Saturn, are in the terms of Jupiter. Saturn dominates the terms, and Saturn himself is completely dominated by Jupiter in rulership, in triplicity and in terms.

Saturn in terms was clearly expressed in how conservative and strict he was, and how much of a disciplinarian he was - his nickname was, Der Panzer Kardinal. Saturn, representing the conservative Roman Catholic church in the ninth house of this chart, was in turn ruled by Jupiter, which in this case is Benedict himself, and also Jupiter/Benedict as representative and embodiment of the church.

Notice that all three of the planets that have dignity in terms here are outer, in the sense of being further away from the Sun than the Earth is. The three together are very rigid and severe.

Robin Williams

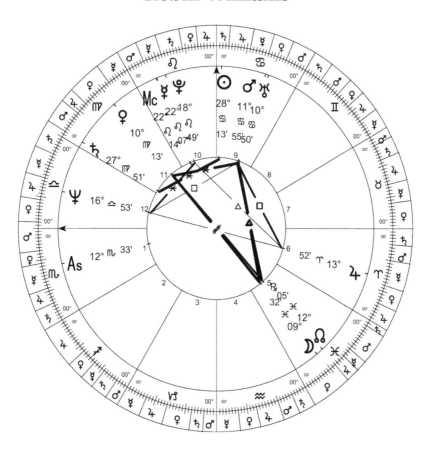

Robin McLaurin Williams, July 21, 1951, 1:34 PM, Chicago, Illinois. Rodden Rating AA. Whole Sign houses.

Here I want to focus on the dignity of terms for two planets.

Notice Mercury, right at that top of the chart, conjunct the Midheaven in the 10th house - easily the most visible planet in the chart. Looking at Mercury's dignity, Mercury is in his own terms. At the same time, both the Ascendant and the Midheaven, along with Jupiter, are in the terms of Mercury - so his self-expression at both of the main angles is in terms of Mercury. It fits.

It is worth looking at Venus which is in its fall in Virgo. Mercury dominates Venus since she is in the sign of Mercury's rulership and exaltation. Venus is a lot stronger than she looks at first glance, though, since she has dignity in triplicity, and term, and face, all three of the minor dignities. Venus is also the next planet after the Midheaven, and I suspect this strong Venus, ruled by Mercury, added to the man's definite charm and charisma. A very strong and competent Venus ruled by Mercury is also appropriate for an actor and creative artist.

Bounds as a Time Lord System: the Bounds and Primary Directions

Hellenistic astrology has different ways of determining what planet is in charge of a particular period of a person's life. These are called time lord systems. When the point being measured enters an area ruled by a planet, that planet is activated as the time lord, responsible for executing the affairs of that area of life during that time period.

Bounds and Prediction

The bounds find their major use in traditional astrology as a time lord system that moves important points, most notably the Ascendant, through the different bounds, noting the lords of the bounds it enters and the aspects it makes. This was referred to as distribution through the bounds, or sometimes as circumambulation through the bounds. I generally refer to it as direction through the bounds - the three words direction, distribution and circumambulation have equivalent meanings.

The chosen point is moved forward in time using primary direction. This is based on the daily rotation of the earth around its axis. Four minutes of clock time, which is 1/360 the length of the day, is taken to be equal to one year of time in the native's life.

The Ascendant is the most common point to direct through the bounds in this way. The distance that the Ascendant moves through the zodiac in four minutes of clock time is referred to as one degree of oblique ascension. It is called oblique because the ecliptic is at an angle relative to the rotation of the earth. Since the slant of the ecliptic varies with the different signs, the oblique ascension of a point varies by sign and by the latitude of the location north or south of the equator. Because of the angle of the ecliptic, one degree of oblique ascension could be more or less than a degree on the ecliptic.

Picture the Ascendant at the eastern horizon, with a specific degree of the zodiac sign rising at the time of birth. As time passes through the day, the successive degrees and signs of the zodiac come up over the horizon and the Ascendant degree changes. That is the movement used in moving the Ascendant forward in time. The distance the Ascendant moves along the ecliptic in four minutes of clock time correlates with one year in the native's life.

As the Ascendant changes degree it moves into the terms of different planets. Whatever term the Ascendant is in is the bound lord or term lord for that period of the person's life.

The following illustration shows a portion of the natal chart of Jimi Hendrix. The dates on the left show when the Ascendant will move into the terms of different planets.

Picture the wheel of zodiac degrees rotating clockwise as it rises over the horizon, which has the effect of moving the Ascendant degree forward in a counter-clockwise direction.

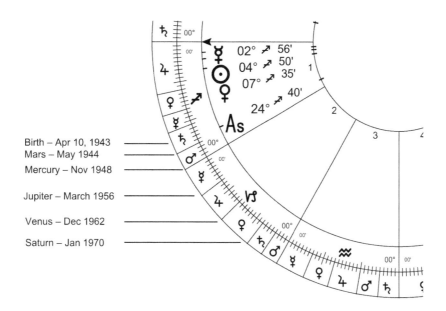

Hendrix was born April 10, 1943, and his Ascendant was in the bounds of Saturn, meaning Saturn was his bound lord at birth. In May 1944 the Ascendant moved into the bounds of Mars, who then took over as time lord through until March 1956, and so on.

For Hendrix, the period of his major success in music came during the mid 1960's, while the Ascendant was in the terms of Venus. In early 1970 the Ascendant went into the terms of Saturn. Hendrix died September 18, 1970.

William Lilly and Directions using the Terms

For an example of the use of the terms in directions, I want to look at William Lilly - I am using the word term here since that is how it appears in Lilly's works. The third book of his *Christian Astrology* is on natal charts, and in the latter half of the book he uses these primary directions with five main points in the chart - the Ascendant, the Midheaven, Sun, Moon, and the Lot of Fortune. Each of these points represents a major area of a person's life, and they were used to determine the general good or ill fortune of the native.

For each of the points, and in his examples, Lilly always notes when the point being directed enters a new division of the terms.

Here are some examples from Lilly describing how the planet ruling the terms the Ascendant is in sets the tone for activities in that period - things are done on that planet's terms.

This quote describes the Ascendant moving into the terms of Saturn.

> *The Native is then usually slow and dull in his actions, little mind to speak, dogged and reserved, full of Envy and Malice, hard to please, waspish, it represents the Native not caring which end goes forward...* (p. 657)

By contrast, here is his description of the Ascendant in the terms of Venus.

> *The Native's Complexion and Disposition inclines to cheerfulnesse, he is active, and much delighted in Women's companies, prone to Musick, Dancing, to all honest and pleasant Sports and Pastimes, happy in the affaires he undertakes, and in his Trade. (p. 662)*

Please see my book, **Direction Through the Bounds in Traditional Astrology**, for further detail and examples of this very important predictive technique. (Projected publication second half of 2018.)

Face

According to James Holden, the dignity of face is of Egyptian origin. The zodiac is divided into 10 degree areas, 3 per sign. Each of the faces was attributed to different gods. The faces are sometimes referred to as decans or decanates from the number ten.

In the Hellenistic system of faces, the ten degree divisions are assigned to the planets in reverse order of their distance from the Earth, as in the following table.

	0°-9°	10°-19°	20°-29°
Aries	Mars	Sun	Venus
Taurus	Mercury	Moon	Saturn
Gemini	Jupiter	Mars	Sun
Cancer	Venus	Mercury	Moon
Leo	Saturn	Jupiter	Mars
Virgo	Sun	Venus	Mercury
Libra	Moon	Saturn	Jupiter
Scorpio	Mars	Sun	Venus
Sagittarius	Mercury	Moon	Saturn
Capricorn	Jupiter	Mars	Sun
Aquarius	Venus	Mercury	Moon
Pisces	Saturn	Jupiter	Mars

Here is another way of picturing the order of the faces. In this chart, the faces are shown in the ring inside the signs, 3 per sign, each taking up 10 degrees. Start the ring at Aries and go counter-clockwise, and note that the planets go in reverse order of their distance from the

69

Earth, from furthest to nearest - Saturn, Jupiter, Mars, Sun, Venus, Mercury, Moon. The series of faces starts with Mars in Aries, and goes in order down through to the Moon, then begins the cycle again with Saturn, Jupiter and so on. The whole series ends with Mars at the end of Pisces.

Decanates from Indian Astrology

Note that there is another system of decanates which is originally from Indian astrology. In that system, the planets are assigned to the decanates using the 3 rulers of the same element in order. For instance, Aries has the decanates assigned to Mars, Sun, and Jupiter, the rulers of the three fire signs, Aries, Leo and Sagittarius.

You will sometimes see this system in modern astrology texts.

	0°-9°	10°-19°	20°-29°
Aries	Mars	Sun	Jupiter
Taurus	Venus	Mercury	Saturn
Gemini	Mercury	Venus	Saturn
Cancer	Moon	Mars	Jupiter
Leo	Sun	Jupiter	Mars
Virgo	Mercury	Saturn	Venus
Libra	Venus	Saturn	Mercury
Scorpio	Mars	Jupiter	Moon
Sagittarius	Jupiter	Mars	Sun
Capricorn	Saturn	Venus	Mercury
Aquarius	Saturn	Mercury	Venus
Pisces	Jupiter	Moon	Mars

In this chart and table the system of decanates from Vedic astrology is shown.

Looking again at Pisces, the three decanates are assigned to Jupiter, Moon and Mars, the rulers of the three water signs, Pisces, Cancer and Moon.

Clearly this is a completely different system from the Hellenistic system of faces. In this book we will be using the Hellenistic system.

To give an idea of how the faces were used in Hellenistic astrology, I want to look at some quotes from traditional writers that talk about the faces.

Historical Quotes

This is from Paul of Alexandria, one of the earliest Hellenistic astrology writers whose works have survived. The emphasis is mine.

> *The faces of the seven stars (planets) which are distributed through the signs from the shaping of the decans, **in which the stars rejoice just as though they were in their own domiciles**, must be worked out in the same order as the heptazone (seven planets in order from Saturn in to the Moon).(p.10)*

This quote suggests the faces were originally used as a separate rulership system. There was not yet any sense of relative ranking or strength of the faces over sign rulership, and they were given equal weight.

This next quote is from the Roman writer Firmicus Maternus.

> *these decans...are assigned to the individual stars, and if a star was in that very decan, even though it is in the domicile of another*, **it must be considered the same as if it were posited in its own domicile.**
> *Some persons...attach three divinities to each decan, termed duty officers. (p.48)*

Another Hellenistic writer, Rhetorius the Egyptian, describes the effect of the faces in the following passage. For Rhetorius the faces show personality traits.

> *Suppose the Sun to be in the 10th degree of Aries, in the first decan, the face of Mars. Since...the Sun signifies the mental characteristics, you will find the mind of this man to be manly, irascible, delighting in war, fond of weapons, and such like.*

> *The Sun...in 20 degrees of Aries, in the second decan, the face of the Sun. It signifies this individual to be magnanimous and loving fame and fond of honor.*

> *The Sun...in the third decan, the face of Venus. It signifies this individual to be womanly in spirit, womanish in appearance, shameful, lustful, and such like.(p.9)*

This next quote from Sahl, one of the most important Arabic astrologers, describes the meaning of the faces in terms of appearance.

> *And know that the first face of Aries ascends the form of a black man wrapped in white clothing. And in the second face ascends the form of a woman upon whom are red cloths. And in the third, the form of a man with pale color, and red hair.(p.118)*

These same descriptions from Sahl also appear in Cornelius Agrippa's *Three Books of Occult Philosophy*, in a section on the magical virtues of the planets.

The next quote is from Avraham Ibn-Ezra, a Jewish traditional astrology writer, working in the same Hellenistic tradition.

> *(In Aries) In the first face there ascends the figure of a radiant woman, and the tail of the Sea-Fish and the form of an ox...*

> *In the second face there ascends fishes, and the middle of the Triangle, and the half of the Animal, and a woman with a comb in her hair, and a bronze armor, and the Head of the Devil.(p. 18-19)*

These descriptions could be referring to associations with the constellations, or to deities associated with that area of the zodiac. That would connect back to a possible Egyptian usage of the faces.

This is another quote from Ibn-Ezra speaking of the meaning of the faces in a different way.

> *(In Aries) One born in the first face will be yellow, with a narrow chest, and little flesh. He has a mark on his left leg and his left arm. His friends are many, and he abhors evil.*
>
> *One born in the second face will be dark, with a handsome face, and his body will be medium. He is short-tempered but does not hold a grudge, with moral integrity, and his enemies are many. (p. 21)*

As with Sahl, these are descriptions of the person based on which face is on the Ascendant at birth.

In a separate text, Ibn-Ezra says that,

> *"A planet in its face is like a person with fine ornaments and clothing." (p. 136)*

Again, we see the connection between face and appearance.

This quote is from Bonatti, from the horary section of his *Book of Astronomy*. In a section talking about finding a thief of stolen goods, the following descriptions of the face are used to give the appearance of the thief.

> *For if the house signifying the thief were the first face of Aries, it signifies that the thief is a man of brown color, and when he steals he is dressed in clothes pertaining more to the color white, than to another color.*
>
> *And if it were the second face of Aries, it signifies that the thief is a woman who then had clothing pertaining more to the color red than to another.*
>
> *And if it were in its third face, it signifies that the thief has a pallid color and has red hair. (p. 477-478)*

This next quote is from Sepharial, an astrology writer from the late 19th century. These descriptions of Aries rising, from the late 19th century, use the face rising at the Ascendant to describe appearance in the sense of personality.

> *1st Decan, ruled by Mars. It confers a warlike and aggressive spirit, a taste for political and public work; disposes to injuries in the head and face...*
>
> *2nd Decan, ruled by Sun. A proud and haughty nature, desiring to bear rule; ambitious and aspiring; extravagant and generous nature...*
>
> *3rd Decan, ruled by Venus. Gives strong passions, love of pleasures; bright and sparkling nature, love of art and poetry; renders the nature very kind and loving,*

but very impulsive and over-ardent. (p.19)

Later Meaning as a Dignity

In the surviving Hellenistic astrology texts face was not widely used. In the system of five essential dignities face is the weakest, and is sometimes omitted.

All of the other essential dignities imply a position of management, control or team membership. Face has a much less important position. If you think of the other dignities as having to do with management or supervision, then face would apply to someone who was a craftsman, or an employee, who has a task to perform but no real control.

This may relate to the connotation of the word face as meaning superficial, appearance only. Face is sometimes used to modify the description or appearance of a point, often of the Ascendant.

By the time of the fully developed system of dignities face had very little weight. The following quotes are from later traditional authors, where they are talking about the dignity of face as the least powerful and important of the series of essential dignities.

This quote is from Bonatti.

> *And when a planet is in its own face, it is like a man who is among unknown people, as sometimes happens to foreigners, and the like, though he lives among them because of an art and profession or service, or because of some other craftsman's or lay art.*

This next quote is from William Lilly.

> *A planet having little or no dignity but by being in his Decanate or face, is almost like a man ready to be turned out of doors, having much ado to maintaine himself in credit and reputation: and in Genealogies it represents a Family at the last gasp, even as good as quite decayed, hardly able to support itself. (p. 103)*

Examples of Face in Charts

In the next few examples we will explore using the dignity of face at the Ascendant and Midheaven of some famous people.

Bob Dylan

Bob Dylan is one of the best known song writers and performers from the turbulent 1960's. His songs are often autobiographical and personal, and the best of his work comes from his personal suffering.

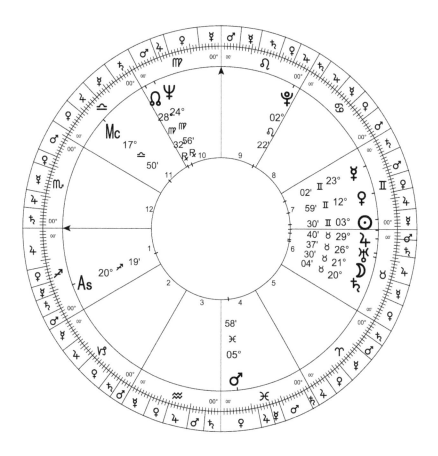

Robert Allen Zimmerman, May 24, 1941, 9:05 PM, Duluth. Minnesota. Rodden Rating AA. Whole Sign houses.

For Dylan both the Ascendant and the Midheaven are in the face of Saturn. Saturn himself is in his face in Taurus, conjunct the Moon.

Dylan has a strong private side. He also made his own depression and emotional suffering (Saturn plus Moon) the subject of much of his best work - it is the face he gives the world. And - he dresses in black!

Dylan produced some of his albums under the name Jack Frost, the dead of winter, which is ruled by Saturn.

Henry Miller

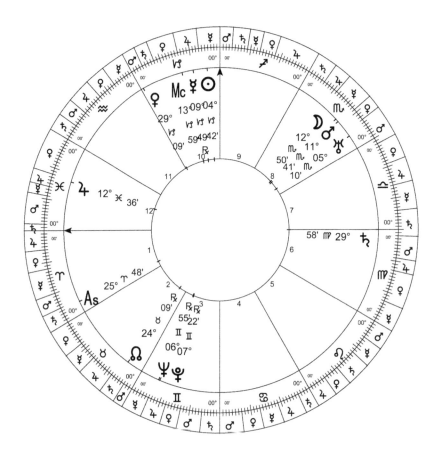

Henry Valentine Miller, December 26, 1891, 12:30 PM, Manhattan, New York. Rodden Rating A. Whole Sign houses.

Henry Miller is best known for *Tropic of Cancer* and other works written in Paris in the 1930's and banned as obscene in America until the 1960's. In the tradition of Whitman and Thoreau, Miller is a modern champion of individual freedom of expression.

For Henry Miller the Midheaven is in the face of Mars, but the Ascendant is in the face of Venus. Miller's public persona was very masculine, but in private and in person he could come across quite sensitive and feminine.

We will have further examples of the use of the dignity of face in later sections.

Note: If you are interested in further historical detail and a different approach to the use of the faces, Austin Coppock's recently published book, *36 Faces*, is worth checking out.

Because of the last gasp, limited control quality of face, Lee Lehman associates it with fear or anxiety. I do not find that meaning to be satisfactory, since it takes a dignity and turns it into more of a debility. Used this way, having dignity by face is more of a debility than being peregrine. To be consistent, if planets with face have fear and anxiety, then peregrine planets should have those qualities more extremely, and I do not find that to be the case.

I would say that since face is such a minor dignity its expression does depend very heavily on the location and condition of its ruling planets. If the support is lacking then having dignity of face can indeed be precarious, but being peregrine without support is much more so. This is face as not being very far removed from peregrine, just one step away.

On the next page is a table of all five of the essential dignities. The table also appears again at the end of the book.

Tables of Essential Dignities

Sign	Ruler	Detriment	Exaltation	Fall	Triplicity			Face		
					Day	Night	Partner	0-9	10-19	20-29
♈	♂	♀	☉	♄	☉	♃	♄	♂	☉	♀
♉	♀	♂	☽		♀	☽	♂	☿	☽	♄
♊	☿	♃			♄	☿	♃	♃	♂	☉
♋	☽	♄	♃	♂	♀	♂	☽	♀	☿	☽
♌	☉	♄			☉	♃	♄	♄	♃	♂
♍	☿	♃	☿	♀	♀	☽	♂	☉	♀	☿
♎	♀	♂	♄	☉	♄	☿	♃	☽	♄	♃
♏	♂	♀		☽	♀	♂	☽	♂	☉	♀
♐	♃	☿			☉	♃	♄	☿	☽	♄
♑	♄	☽	♂	♃	♀	☽	♂	♃	♂	☉
♒	♄	☉			♄	☿	♃	♀	☿	☽
♓	♃	☿	♀	☿	♀	♂	☽	♄	♃	♂

Bounds or Terms

♈	0	♃	6	♀	12	☿	20	♂	25	♄
♉	0	♀	8	☿	14	♃	22	♄	27	♂
♊	0	☿	6	♃	12	♀	17	♂	24	♄
♋	0	♂	7	♀	13	☿	18	♃	26	♄
♌	0	♃	6	♀	11	♄	18	☿	24	♂
♍	0	☿	7	♀	17	♃	21	♂	28	♄
♎	0	♄	6	☿	14	♃	21	♀	28	♂
♏	0	♂	7	♀	11	☿	19	♃	24	♄
♐	0	♃	12	♀	17	☿	21	♄	26	♂
♑	0	☿	7	♃	14	♀	22	♄	26	♂
♒	0	☿	7	♀	13	♃	20	♂	25	♄
♓	0	♀	12	♃	16	☿	19	♂	28	♄

The degree in the term table is the degree that bound starts.
For instance, Venus term in Aries begins at 6 degrees.

Using the Essential Dignities Together

In using the five essential dignities, look for overall patterns. They are most useful considered within the overall context of the chart, especially where one or two planets predominate.

Look at planetary dignity in the chart as a whole. Any planet that dominates in overall dignity has great influence and responsibility.

Look for predominance of a planet within a single dignity. With triplicity this aligns with elemental balance. For instance, if the majority of the planets and angles in a chart are in fire and air, the planets Sun, Saturn and Jupiter will have increased importance and influence.

If one or two planets dominate the bounds, that planet will be particularly significant in how the person acts in the world, how they implement their goals. We saw that with Mercury in the chart of Maya Angelou.

The Minor dignities are also very important with planets in aspect, to determine how well they work together.

The Ascendant and Midheaven have primary importance, so all of the dignities at those points are worth checking. I particularly consider bound or term at the angles since it shows implementation and style of acting.

Here is an example of examining predominance of dignity with the chart of Ted Turner, the billionaire founder of CNN, who has had a profound influence on the development of Internet media news.

Ted Turner

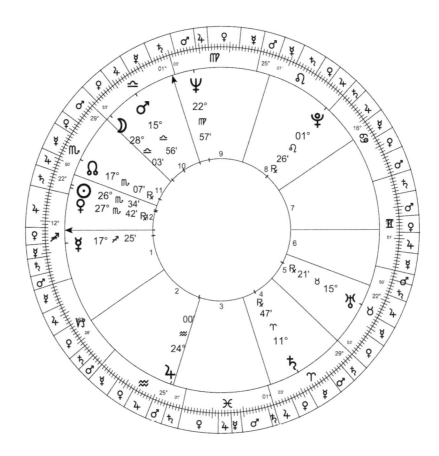

Robert Edward Turner. November 19, 1938, 8:50 AM, Cincinnati, Ohio. Rodden Rating AA. Placidus house system.

"Early to bed, early to rise, work like hell and advertise." - Ted Turner

The dominant aspect pattern is the strong angular opposition between Mars and Saturn, tenth to fourth houses. Mars is in detriment in Libra, and Saturn is in fall. This does not look very auspicious at first glance. But, notice - Mars and Saturn have a strong mixed reception, with Saturn in the rulership of Mars, and Mars in the exaltation of Saturn. Mutual reception like this abates all malice, it takes away any ill will or antagonism between the planets. Even with the tension of the opposition the planets regard each other well and are motivated to work together. This opposition with major reception generates enormous energy.

There are two other planets that are related to the opposition that form a powerful aspect pattern to smooth and harmonize its expression.

Mercury, in Sagittarius, is angular and rising within five degrees of the Ascendant, and Mercury makes a trine to Saturn and a sextile to Mars.

Jupiter, the ruler of the Ascendant, is in Aquarius. By sign, it makes a loose trine to Mars, a sextile to Saturn, and a sextile to Mercury.

Three of the four planets in this configuration are the dominant angular planets of the chart.

Here we will analyze the dignity of the planets to see how well they will work together, and which planet or planets predominate within the pattern.

Pl	Ruler	Exalt	Tripl	Term	Face	Detri	Fall
☉	♂	--	♀♂☽	♄	♀	♀	☽
☽	♀	♄	♄☿♃	♂	♃ m	♂	☉
☿	♃	☋	☉♃♄	☿ +	☽	☿ -	--
♀	♂ m	--	♀♂☽ +	♄ m	♀ +	♀ -	☽
♂	♀ m	♄	♄☿♃	♃ m	♄	♂ -	☉
♃	♄	--	♄☿♃ +	♂ m	☽ m	☉	--
♄	♂	☉	☉♃♄ +	♀ m	☉	♀	♄ -
☊	♂	--	♀♂☽	☿	☉	♀	☽
⊗	♂	--	♀♂☽	☿	☉	♀	☽
As	♃	☋	☉♃♄	♀	☽	☿	--
Mc	♀	♄	♄☿♃	♄	☽	♂	☉
☋	♀	☽	♀☽♂	♃	☽	♂	--

Starting with Saturn, the Sun predominates in dignity. Along with the mutual reception with Mars, Saturn has dignity by triplicity, the family or group dignity, as does Jupiter.

Mars is dominated by Saturn, having Saturn in exaltation, triplicity and face. Mars also has Jupiter by triplicity, and has a mutual reception by term with Jupiter. Planets in mutual reception by term work well together.

Mercury is in detriment, but is in its own terms, which makes it competent to act. Mercury has Jupiter as ruler and in triplicity, and has Saturn in triplicity.

Jupiter is dominated by Saturn in rulership and triplicity. Jupiter is in its own triplicity, and has mutual reception with Mars by term.

If you put these all together, a pattern emerges.

Saturn dominates the pattern as a whole, and both Saturn and Jupiter have dignity at all four points of this configuration.

Also, Saturn and Jupiter both have reception from Mars.

Saturn, dominant planet here, is in the fourth house of ancestry and family.

Saturn is Ted Turner's father.

The Saturn /Mars opposition describes their complex and tense relationship, and Jupiter and Mercury show ways that the relationship was worked out in his life. That opposition, that relationship, is the fuel that drove Ted Turner.

Here is some information on Ted Turner and his father from biographical information on the internet.

Ted's father owned his own company, Turner Advertising... Although Ed was a good provider, he suffered from mood swings caused by bipolar disorder and vented his anger by physically abusing Ted. Years later, as an adult, Ted would discover he too was bipolar.

In 1960, Ted's father made him the manager of Turner Advertising's Macon, Georgia, branch. Ted quickly showed a natural talent for business by more than doubling the office's revenue in his first year. When Turner's father bought out a competitor in 1962, the costly buyout and subsequent debt placed the company in a tenuous financial condition. Fearing bankruptcy and struggling to cope with bipolar disorder, Ed shot himself to death in March of 1963. Ted dealt with his grief by throwing himself into his work. He took over the roles of president and chief executive officer at Turner Advertising.

Saturn, Mars, Mercury, Jupiter.

We mentioned earlier that Saturn is dominated in dignities by the Sun. The Sun in this chart is peregrine in Scorpio in the twelfth house of self-undoing - Ted's father shot and killed himself.

Note also the following house connections relative to his work.

Mercury, rising at the Ascendant, rules Virgo, the ninth house, and Neptune is in Virgo. Ninth house can relate to global media, and Neptune is related to media.

Saturn and Mars are both strong in Capricorn in the second house, with Saturn as ruler and Mars in exaltation and triplicity. **Saturn and Mars combine rulership in the house of finances.**

Predominance of dignity in this aspect configuration clearly shows the dominant planets in this chart and how they work together.

Supporting Techniques

To use dignities and debilities well there are some important supporting techniques and concepts that we need to have in place.

Disposition

This is related to the major dignity of rulership. When a planet rules a house, it disposes of the affairs of that house. To dispose of is to take care of, to see that it is handled. The terms ruler and dispositor are synonyms.

Dispositor Chain

The dispositor chain refers to the chain of command that marks who a planet reports to, and who that planet reports to in turn, and so on up until a planet is reached that is in its own house or rulership, or until the chain circles back on itself.

Final Dispositor

You have a final chart dispositor only in the situation where only a single planet is in its rulership, and all other planets trace their chain of command back to that one planet. When a chart does have a final dispositor, that planet takes on exceptional importance and responsibility as it basically gives orders to all the other planets, directly and indirectly.

Bob Dylan

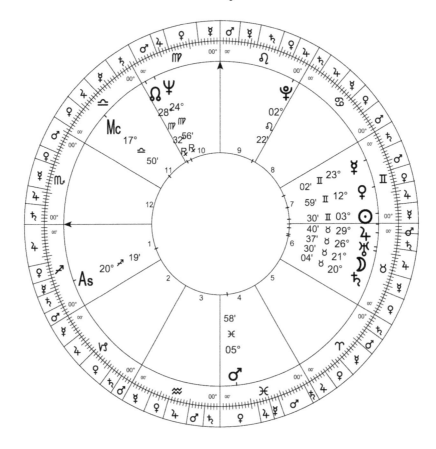

Robert Allen Zimmerman, May 24, 1941, 9:05 PM, Duluth. Minnesota. Rodden Rating AA. Whole Sign houses.

In Bob Dylan's chart, Mercury is the only planet in rulership, in Gemini in the 7th house. All other planets in the chart trace their rulership back to Mercury, as in the diagram at the right.

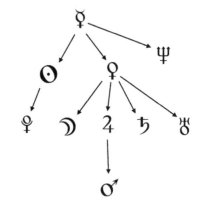

Pair Final Dispositor

Sometimes you will find charts that trace the chain of dispositors back to a pair of planets, each of which is in the other's rulership. In the tradition of western astrology, only a single planet final dispositor would be recognized. I have found it is worth considering that pair as shared final dispositors, where their interaction sets the tone for the chart.

Dane Rudhyar

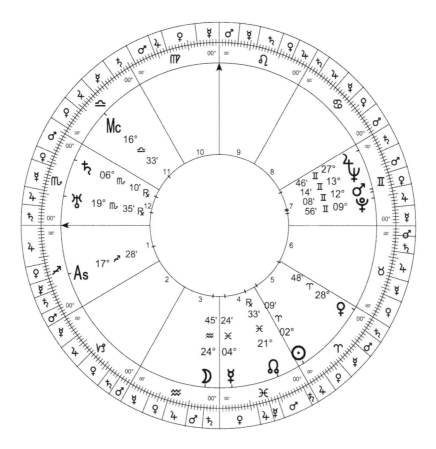

Daniel Chenneviere, March 23, 1895, 1 AM, Paris, France. Rodden Rating AA. Whole Sign houses.

In Dane Rudhyar's chart, no planets are in the sign of their own rulership. Mercury is in Pisces, and Jupiter is in Gemini, so they have mutual reception by rulership. All of the other planets trace their rulership back to those two planets. I do not think you could find a more appropriate combination or ruling planets for a philosopher, astrologer, writer and composer.

For a further example of mutual co-dispositors, see the chart of Pope Francis in the examples section of this book.

Aspects and Dignities

The relationship between a planet and a house or other point where it has essential dignity determines its effectiveness. Traditional astrology requires that the ruling planet have an aspect by whole sign to the house it rules in order to effectively influence and control the house. The aspect indicates that the ruler can see and communicate with its house.

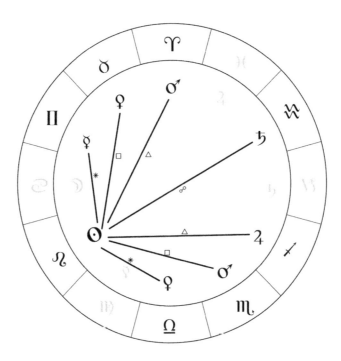

The black lines drawn in this diagram from the Sun show the traditional or ptolemaic aspects - conjunction, sextile, square, trine and opposition. A planet can see and communicate with any other planet where there is a whole sign aspect between them.

Aversion

In the diagram above, the Sun in Leo has no whole sign aspect to the grayed out signs. (The averse signs are either one sign or five signs away, and are comparable to the modern semisextile and qunincunx aspects.) Those signs are said to be in aversion, meaning the planet can't see them, they are outside of the planet's line of vision. The word averse means turned away.

A planet in aspect to a house can see it, communicate with it, be in touch with it. A planet averse to a house is like an absentee landlord – it is out of touch, it cannot see the house it rules. When considering dignity, it is important to note both the condition of the planet and whether it aspects the point it rules.

Second House Lords Averse

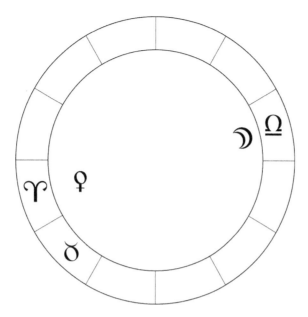

In this example the second house is Taurus, and the two main rulers, Venus (ruler of Taurus) is in Aries one sign away, and the Moon (exalted in Taurus) in Libra five signs away, are averse to Taurus. This can play out as a lack of awareness and control in the area of personal finances.

Antiscia

Planets in antiscia are an equal distance from the Cancer/Capricorn axis. In the diagram below, a point in Gemini can be in antiscia to Cancer, Taurus to Leo, Aries to Virgo, and so on. Think of the Cancer/Capricorn line as an axis of reflection like a mirror. Points in antiscia have a kind of conjunction by reflection across this axis.

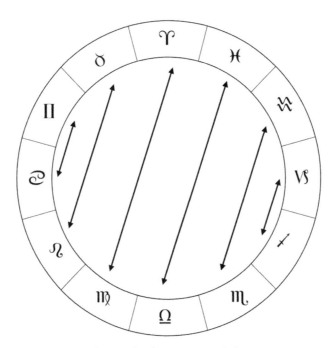

For example, a planet at 12⁰ Taurus is Antiscia one at 18 ⁰ Leo.

The point opposite an Antiscia point is called a contrantiscia.

Planets in antiscia act like a conjunction; in contrantiscia, like an opposition. I think of it as a shadow or reflection aspect, and it often has a behind-the-scenes quality to it. Both antiscia and contrantiscia aspects strongly link the planets together, but in a way that is often hidden.

I have found that up to 2 or 3 degree orbs for antiscia can have a significant effect.

Table of Antiscia Signs

Sign	Antiscia	
Cancer	Gemini	Note that you can read the signs in order by going down the left column, and then up the right column. The signs reflect across the Cancer / Capricorn axis.
Leo	Taurus	
Virgo	Aries	
Libra	Pisces	
Scorpio	Aquarius	
Sagittarius	Capricorn	

To find the antiscia of a point, find the matching sign in this table, and take its degree position and subtract it from 30⁰. For instance, the antiscia of 8⁰ Pisces 45" is 21⁰ Libra 15". The contra-antiscia is opposite the antiscia - in this case, 21⁰ Aries 15".

Gloria Steinem

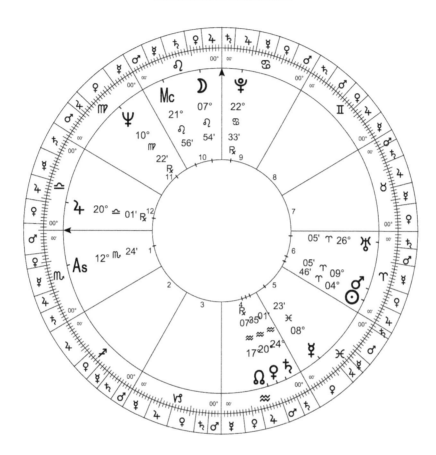

Gloria Marie Steinem, March 25, 1934, 10 PM, Toledo, Ohio. Rodden Rating AA. Whole Sign houses.

Gloria Steinem is a very well known feminist leader, activist, writer, and the founder and editor of Ms. Magazine.

Mercury is peregrine, in detriment and fall in Pisces. Every one of Mercury's rulers is averse. This woman is a writer and magazine editor, so clearly Mercury is getting support somewhere.

Note that Mercury and Jupiter are conjunct by Antiscia within about a degree and a half orb.

Examining the full system of dignities, Jupiter has dignity by triplicity, term and face, so it is a lot stronger than it looks at first glance. Further, there is a mutual mixed reception here - Jupiter receives Mercury by rulership, and is received by Mercury by triplicity. Given the antiscia relationship with the mutual reception it is clear that the two planets can support each other.

89

Marilyn Monroe

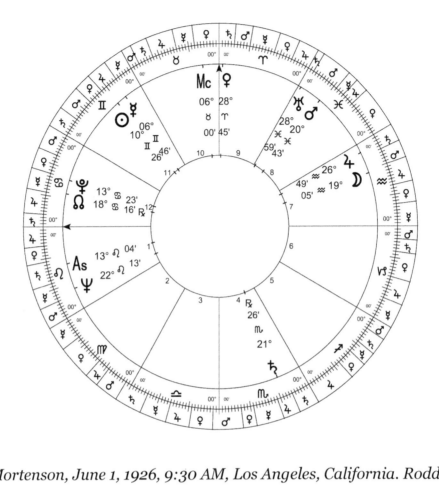

Norma Jean Mortenson, June 1, 1926, 9:30 AM, Los Angeles, California. Rodden Rating AA.

The planet I want to consider here is Neptune, which is very strong in the first house at 22 Leo 13 and is rising. Note that the antiscia of Neptune is at 7 Taurus 47, which is a bit less than two degrees orb from Midheaven at 6 Taurus 01.

Neptune, the planet of illusion and glamour, is conjunct the Ascendant, and is also conjunct the Midheaven by antiscia. Neptune dominates Monroe's visibility in the public eye, and her life became a media created illusion that had very little to do with the real Norma Jean behind the media mask.

Almuten

The word almuten is from the Arabic *al-mubtazz*, victor or winner. The almuten is the planet that has the most influence at a given point in overall dignity. When looking for the almuten, take into account things like planetary condition, and aspects.

Almuten Example

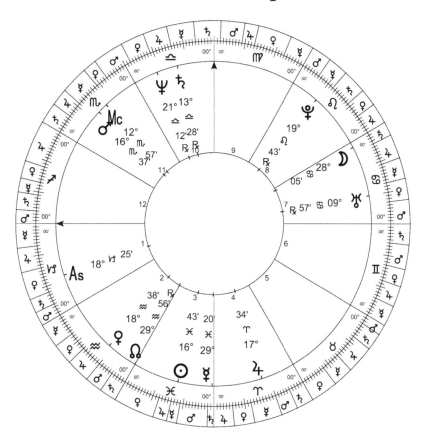

This is my birth chart.

The Ascendant in this chart is at 18 Capricorn, which is ruled by Saturn. However, at this degree, Mars has dignity by exaltation, triplicity and face. Clearly, Mars is the almuten of the Ascendant since it has more dignity there than does Saturn. Both Saturn and Mars closely aspect the Ascendant so both planets will be influential, but the influence of Mars will likely end up being dominant.

Allen Ginsberg

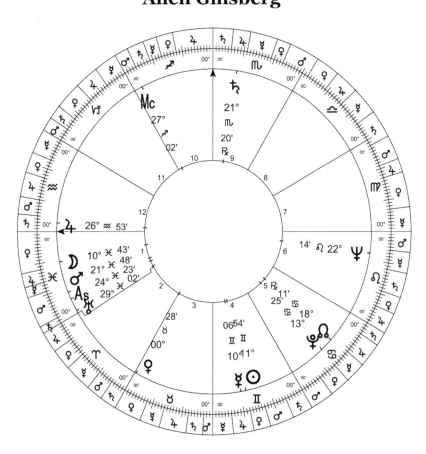

Irwin Allen Ginsberg, June 3, 1926, 2 am, Newark, New Jersey. Rodden Rating A. Whole Sign houses.

The planet to look at here is Mars, which is conjunct the Ascendant. At first glance, Mars does not look to be particularly strong by essential dignity. Yet, if you use the whole system of dignities, Mars has dignity by triplicity and term and face, so its cumulative dignity is very strong. The Ascendant is also in the triplicity, term and face of Mars, so Mars is the almuten or dominant planet of the Ascendant. Being conjunct the Ascendant it will clearly dominate here.

Peregrine

With the concept of dignity or assigned role, there needs to be a way of dealing with a planet that has no dignities. This is the concept of peregrine. The word means wanderer or stranger. A peregrine planet is homeless, it has no assigned place and no rights.

A peregrine planet very much depends on the condition and aspects of the planets that rule its location to be able to function. It is a guest at the mercy of its hosts.

Consider the following quote from Bonatti.

> *Look to see whether a planet is peregrine, because then it signifies that he...will be clever, astute, malicious - for he will know how to do good and evil, and how to advance cleverly in all action which he wished; however, his intention will be more inclined toward evil than to good.*

This is peregrine as "street smart", a homeless outsider used to living by their wits. Peregrine planets are not necessarily loyal to the same rules as the "insiders". The survival skills of peregrine planets can be assets.

Peregrine in Horary vs. Natal

There is a difference in interpretation of peregrine planets in horary astrology compared to natal. In horary a peregrine planet is considered to not be able to perform at all, so it cannot complete a given task. Peregrine is used in horary in other specific ways – for example, in a horary on theft a peregrine planet in the seventh house is considered to show the thief.

In natal interpretation you need to take into account the processes of growth, experience and choice. Over time, a peregrine planet can get used to functioning in its situation and can become a useful asset - an acclimation takes place.

With peregrine planets it is especially important to consider the planet's rulers, since a peregrine planet relies on its rulers to function. You will likely see the planet's functioning is strongly influenced by its most powerful ruler. This will likely be the ruling planet in the best condition, that aspects the peregrine planet in the most favorable way.

Gloria Steinem

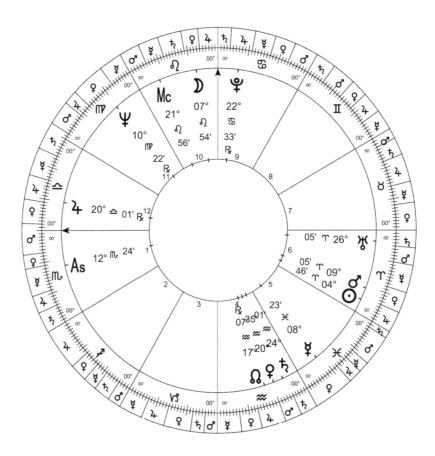

Gloria Marie Steinem, March 25, 1934, 10 PM, Toledo, Ohio. Rodden Rating AA. Whole Sign houses.

The Moon in Gloria Steinem's chart is peregrine. It is in Leo in the 10th house so its action will likely be visible and prominent. The Moon's ruler, the Sun, is exalted and conjunct Mars in rulership. The expression of that Moon will be dominated by its ruler. There is a need the Moon to shine and to be visible in a solar kind of way in the public eye. In this case the sensitivity and receptivity of the Moon will likely be overpowered by its Sun ruler.

Deepak Chopra

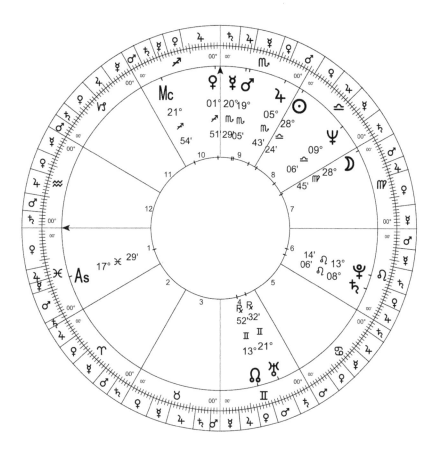

Deepak Chopra, October 12, 1946, 3:45 pm, New Delhi, India. Rodden Rating A. Whole Sign houses.

The planet I want to focus on here is Mercury. It is peregrine at 19 Scorpio and is in the 9th house of religion, philosophy, publishing and teaching. In this case Mercury is conjunct its ruler, Mars, which is very strong in Scorpio. The two planets are further strengthened by having the benefic Jupiter in the same sign and house. Clearly Mercury works well for Chopra, as he is a best-selling author and teacher.

Peregrine and the Dignity system

I think that the concept of peregrine only works if you use the full system of 5 major and minor dignities. Using just the major dignities greatly increases the frequency of peregrine planets. I think that dilutes the significance of the condition. I suggest you use peregrine only with the full five dignity system.

Reception

Reception is one of the most important interpretive principles in traditional astrology. Looking at reception between planets will give you a wealth of information as to how well the planets will interact.

Here is the core concept.

Reception is a statement about the relationship between a planet and the ruler of the sign it occupies. The ruler is said to receive the planet.

Classical reception requires that the ruler can see the sign it rules. Aversion, which is the lack of an aspect, breaks reception in the strict traditional sense.

Reception with an Aspect

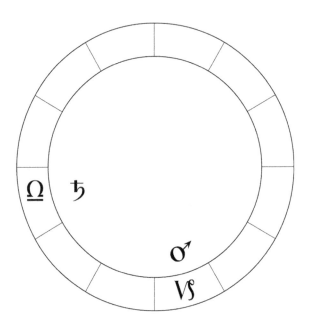

In this diagram Mars is in Capricorn and Saturn is in Libra. Both planets are in the signs of their exaltation and they are in a square aspect by whole sign.

From the point of view of Saturn, Mars is in Capricorn which is a sign Saturn rules; Saturn receives Mars in his house. Mars is staying in a house owned by Saturn, so Saturn has the obligation of a host to treat Mars well.

Looking at this aspect from the point of view of Mars, note that Saturn is in the sign Libra where Mars is in detriment. Mars does not receive Saturn here, so Mars has no obligation to treat Saturn well at all. In fact, Saturn is in a sign where Mars is in detriment, so Mars is likely to treat Saturn poorly. The relationship of Mars to Saturn is not indifferent, it is negative, hostile.

Since each planet is in its own exaltation they are each dignified on their own, and thus function well. The reception modifies their attitude and action on each other. If one or the other of the planets were debilitated this would harm their overall functioning as well as their interaction.

Just saying that Saturn is square Mars gives you very limited information. Adding that Saturn receives Mars in rulership, and Mars does not receive Saturn since Saturn is in the sign of the detriment of Mars, gives you much more information on how the planets are likely to act on each other. Considering each planet's dignity separately adds yet more detail.

Reception with Aversion

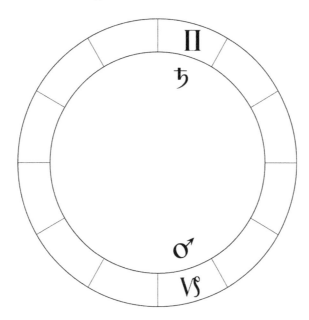

Here Mars is again in Capricorn but Saturn is in Gemini. As in the previous diagram Saturn receives Mars in his house, but there is no whole sign aspect between them - Saturn is averse the house it rules here. Aversion means that the two planets cannot see each other; there is a lack of awareness and communication.

In traditional astrology this is not full reception because of that lack of communication.

Saturn is like an absentee landlord - Mars is staying in a house ruled by Saturn and Saturn isn't aware Mars is there. (Note that the concept of reception was developed before the days of global cell phone coverage, when you could actually have people who were not instantly in touch with each other. I know, it's hard to believe people ever lived that way...)

Aspect without Reception

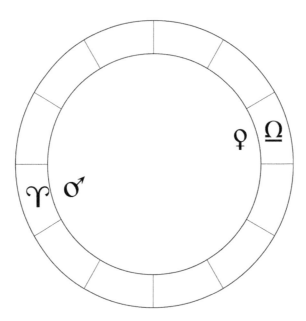

Here Mars is in Aries and Venus is in Libra. Each planet is in a sign it rules, so each of them are happy being in their own home. The two planets are opposite each other by whole sign.

In terms of their relationship, Venus is in the detriment of Mars, and Mars is in the detriment of Venus. Each is in a house where the other does not feel at home, so there is no mutual obligation and little common understanding between them.

There is no reception, obligation or good will here; there is likely hostility and misunderstanding. Because of that lack of reception, this will likely be a difficult aspect relationship.

Strictly speaking there is no concept of negative reception in traditional astrology. In this case, where each planet is in the other's detriment, I think the relation is more negative than if there were a simple lack of reception between them.

Mutual Reception

The optimal relationship between planets is where each is in one of the other's dignities. This is called mutual reception, and it is a statement of mutual support, mutual obligation, mutual respect, mutual understanding.

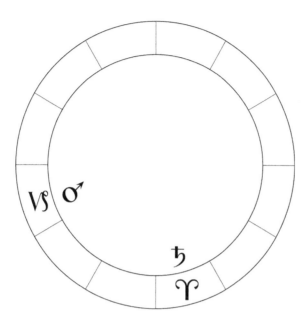

Mars is in Capricorn, a sign ruled by Saturn. Saturn is in Aries, a sign ruled by Mars. The two planets are in a square aspect by whole sign.

Saturn receives Mars in a house he rules, and Mars receives Saturn in a house he rules. This means that they are each obligated to treat the other well.

In William Lilly's words, **_mutual reception abates all malice_**. There is no ill will of any kind between these two planets despite their square aspect, and each has the obligation of host to the other.

Being in exaltation in Capricorn, Mars is in much better shape than Saturn in Aries where he is in his fall, so Mars is likely to be the more helpful planet in this mutual reception.

I have found that when there is major reception between two planets in a chart they will likely play a critical role in tying the whole chart together.

While mutual reception is preferable with an aspect, I have found that mutual reception with averse planets can be important. Mutual reception with aversion can indicate the relationship is outside the person's awareness or control. However, it can still have a positive effect. The mutual reception by itself is enough to create a beneficial relationship between the two planets. We will see an example of that later in this chapter.

Here are examples of reception.

Alexander Graham Bell

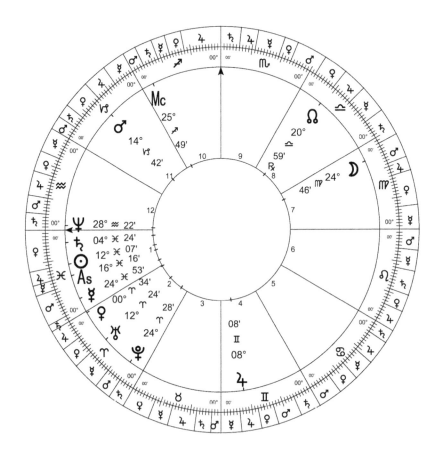

Alexander Graham Bell, March 3, 1847, Edinburgh, Scotland. Rodden Rating AA. Whole Sign houses.

In this chart, Mercury is rising in Pisces, in detriment and fall. Jupiter is in Gemini, in detriment, so both planets have a debility. However, Mercury and Jupiter are in each other's signs. They have mutual reception, and they are in a square aspect by whole sign.

Jupiter rules the Ascendant and the Midheaven so it is a dominant planet in the chart.

One way that planets being out of dignity can work out, is by giving a perspective outside of the accepted or ordinary. In modern slang, planets in detriment can "think outside of the box". Bell was a scientist who invented the telephone.

Steve Allen

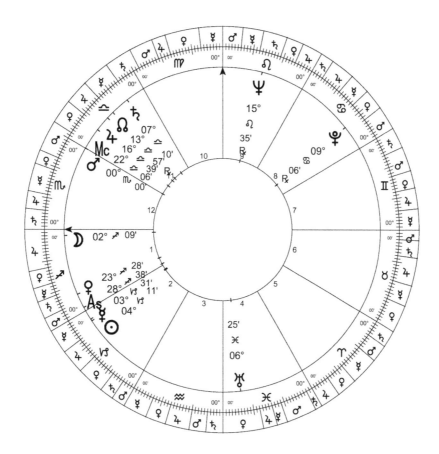

Stephen Valentine Patrick William Allen, December 21, 1921, 7 AM, New York, New York. Rodden Rating A. Whole Sign houses.

This is the chart of Steve Allen - Entertainer, Musician, Comic.

In this chart, Jupiter is conjunct the Midheaven, and Venus is conjunct the Ascendant. Being angular they will dominate the chart. Venus and Jupiter are in each other's signs in mutual reception, and rule both the main angles. Allen has the two benefics in mutual reception. This plays out as Allen being a charming, witty and gracious talk show host, and a fine jazz pianist.

Adolf Hitler

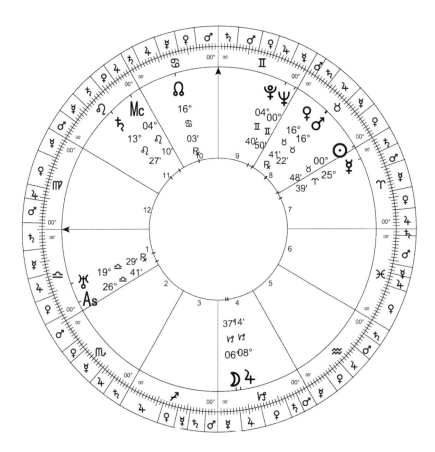

Adolf Hitler, April 20, 1889, 6:30 PM, Braunau, Austria. Rodden Rating AA. Whole Sign houses.

In Hitler's chart, Saturn is in detriment and angular, near the Midheaven in the eleventh house. Mars is in detriment and conjunct the Ascendant ruler Venus. Saturn and Mars are in a tight fixed square, and there is no reception between them at all.

We have the two malefics, Saturn and Mars, both in detriment with no reception, so they are working at cross purposes. This is a constant negative stress from their fixed sign square. Neither planet is getting any help from the other.

Aspects, Dignity and Reception

Use dignities to judge the nature and quality of interaction between two aspecting planets. Take into account both the nature of aspect and the nature of any receptions between the planets.

The optimal condition is mutual reception, meaning each receives the other into some dignity. Mutual reception in major dignities or with multiple minor dignities is particularly strong.

Mixed mutual reception - planets receiving each other in different dignities - seems to work just fine. William Lilly uses mixed mutual reception in his examples.

It is also worth paying attention to the lack of aspects between a planet and its rulers.

In traditional material you will commonly see that reception is considered to improve the quality of an otherwise difficult aspect, and lack of reception makes a difficult aspect worse. For instance, an opposition without reception is about a negative an aspect as you can find, while an opposition with reception can work out well, though not without problems and delays. Similarly a square with reception can indicate cooperation, while a square without reception will be very negative. A positive aspect like a trine or sextile will have a positive effect, and reception greatly strengthens it. Reception upgrades the quality of the aspect, and lack of reception downgrades it.

Herman Melville

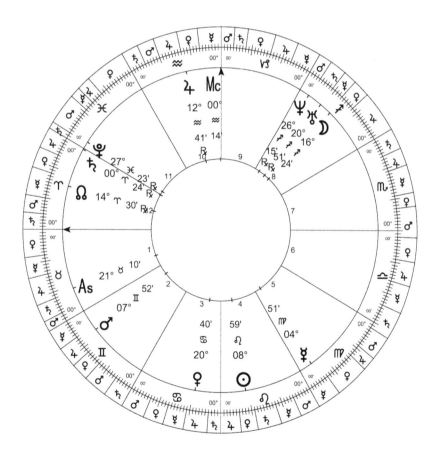

Herman Melville, August 1, 1819, 11:30 PM, New York, New York. Rodden Rating AA. Whole Sign houses.

In Herman Melville's chart, Mercury makes a tight square to Mars. Mars is the planet rising, so he should be visible in the face Melville presents to the world. Mercury is in his rulership in Virgo and Mars is peregrine, so Mercury is very much the stronger planet. Mercury receives Mars in rulership, triplicity and face. Mars in turn receives Mercury in triplicity. Mercury dominates the relationship, but with triplicity reception Mars at least acknowledges Mercury as a member of the same family.

The reception helps the two planets work together, so this square likely works out to his advantage. I think this is visible as Melville the adventurer and story-teller, a sailor who spent time on whaling ships who then wrote novels recounting his adventures, real and imaginary. This is masculine writing, and I think that Mars is quite visible in his style and subject matter.

I want to end this section on reception with a more extended example, looking at mutual reception and aversion together with the minor dignity of face.

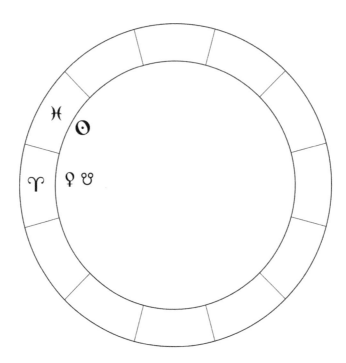

This example is from the chart of a friend of mine, a person I know pretty well and also admire. I am including only the portion of the chart that applies to our example interpretation.

Aries is the Ascendant, and is the first house in this chart. Venus is in the first house, in detriment. Venus also has dignity by face.

Venus is also conjunct the South Node. In traditional astrology the South Node is considered to be of the nature of Saturn, and it diminishes or sucks the energy out of any planet that is near it. Venus here in the first house manifests as this person being somewhat shy and self-effacing.

The other planet we are considering here is the Sun, which is in Pisces in the 12th house. The

Sun is peregrine in Pisces meaning it has no dignity or assigned place, and it is in the very self-effacing and invisible 12th house.

Looking at the planets together, note that Venus and Sun have mutual reception by exaltation – Sun is exalted in Aries where Venus is, and Venus is exalted in Pisces where the Sun is. The two planets value and support each other, so their mutual influence is strengthening.

Notice how the self-effacing quality of Venus is reinforced by her being conjunct the South Node, and also being in mutual reception with the Sun in the self-effacing 12th house.

However, the two planets are also averse, meaning they do not have any whole sign aspect, so they don't see each other. There is something about their relationship that is out of awareness or control. There is no direct conscious communication between the two planets.

Now we will look at how the dignity of face fits here.

In the full system of two major and three minor dignities all of the dignities other than face have some sense of control or responsibility, and there is a domain and level of life where they have power. By contrast, with the minor dignity of face you have an assigned place, but it has no power, no clout, no authority. It can mean something superficial, an appearance or face you are putting on, or it can mean a situation in which you perform a service but don't have any authority – like a volunteer position.

In addition, Venus in detriment – so not at home, not in control, or in an environment where Venus is off-balance or doesn't fit that well.

Now let's put it all together.

The Sun is in the 12th house, which is a house of self-sacrifice, self-undoing. It can also signify work in some kind of institution or environment where people are confined – a prison, a care facility, a hospital, a nursing home. Or, it can also signify work with people in that situation.

Sun in the 12th house can also express as self-sacrifice, self-giving. In mutual reception with Venus in the first, that would mean this person expresses herself in self-sacrificing sorts of ways. With the two planets being averse, this self-sacrificing quality is mostly out of the person's awareness – she doesn't realize how very giving and unselfish a person she is.

Specifically, with mutual reception by exaltation – exaltation has less to do with power, and more to do with value or reputation, or recognition. In this case, qualities having to do with self-giving, self-sacrifice, self-obliteration, are highly valued, highly exalted, by this person. Her sense of self (first house Venus) and her self-sacrificing values (twelfth house Sun) are blended together in the mutual reception.

Venus in face plays out as her doing volunteer work where she has no authority or recognition. With Venus in detriment, this work is in an environment, or a group of people, where she is not at home.

This person does a lot of volunteer work, and one of her positions involved working in a support group for convicted sex offenders who had served prison time. That ties in Venus in detriment, and in ties in the twelfth house self-sacrificing tendency, and the connection between the twelfth house and prisons.

Venus in the first house in mutual reception with Sun in the twelfth house – the person is very self-giving – but the two planets are averse – I am pretty sure she is not aware of just how unselfish and giving she really is.

Venus in her first house expresses in a face sort of position where she is a volunteer with no authority or recognition, in detriment, where she does not really fit in with the people she works with.

The mix of all these different conditions – aversion, mutual reception, dignity by face, and debility by detriment – all combine to describe this part of her life situation very well.

Accidental Dignity

The essential dignities are all defined by zodiac location. At a given moment in time the essential dignities are the same for every person anywhere on earth.

There is another category of conditions, called Accidental dignities, that have an effect on the condition of a planet, and of the ability of planet to perform. Unlike the essential dignities, many of the accidental dignities depend on the specific location on earth at a given moment in time.

As a very general rule, essential dignity is a measure of the quality or condition of the planet and accidental dignity is a measure of the prominence and activity of a planet, its opportunity to act in the world.

This is an oversimplification. Working with the dignities in the context of chart it will quickly become evident that the actual situation is more complex and subtle. Essential dignity can affect strength, and accidental dignity can greatly affect quality.

We will consider the most important accidental dignities in the following sections.

Angularity

In early western astrology angularity is the most important factor to evaluate the strength or weakness of a planet. The charts from Dorotheus that we looked at for evaluating the triplicity rulers of the sect light used angularity as the sole measure of how fortunate or unfortunate a planet's action would be.

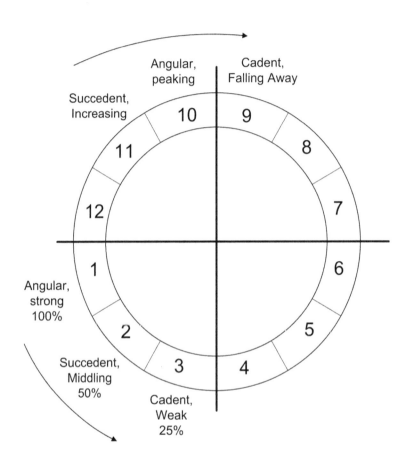

The four angles of the chart, also the called pivots or stakes, are the points of visibility and power. A planet near or in an angular house is strong and visible, and can act with great effectiveness. A planet in a succedent house is not as strong as if it were angular, but is still considered to be positive. A planet in a cadent house is thought to be weak, hidden, weakening, turning inward. Being in an angular house is considered to strengthen a planet and to be fortunate, while being in a cadent house is considered to be a debility.

In the lower left quadrant of the diagram above you have an angular house first, at 100% strength. Next is a succedent house at half of that, 50% strength. Finally, the cadent house is half that again, at 25% strength.

At the top of the diagram, we are looking at the three houses in the order that the planets move through them in their daily motion around the earth. In the succedent eleventh house the planet is approaching the angle and is increasing in strength. The angular tenth house is nearest to the angle of the Midheaven and is at peak strength. In the ninth house the planet is falling away from its peak of power at the Midheaven and is rapidly decreasing in strength.

The word cadent literally means falling away, and it was named from this daily motion of planets first approaching an angle as a rising to a peak, then passing the angle as a descent with a rapid drop in power.

I used the tenth house and Midheaven in the above example showing peaking, but all four of the angles are considered to be peaks of strength.

Along with being a measure of a planet's strength, angularity also relates to visibility in the world. The four angles are where the chart interfaces with the world around us, and angular planets are very visible, which is why they are powerful. Succedent houses are less visible, and cadent houses are considered to be hidden, away from the public view. Planets in cadent houses can have a private, withdrawn, introspective kind of quality, and much of the processing that goes on there is internal.

Good and Bad Houses

In weighing house strength and favorableness, there is a division into good and bad houses. Houses 1, 10, 5 and 11 are considered fortunate or good houses. Houses 6, 8 and 12 are considered unfortunate or bad houses. Houses 2, 3, 4, 7 and 9 are considered mixed, and can go either way.

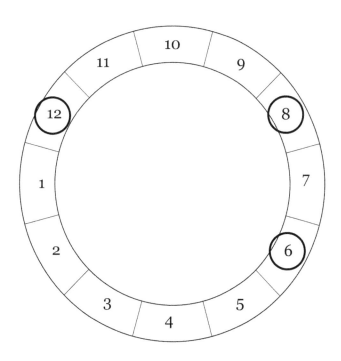

In this diagram the three circled houses are the ones that are considered to be unfortunate. Note that all of these unfortunate houses are averse the Ascendant, meaning that there is no traditional whole sign aspect between the Ascendant and these houses. They are areas that are out of awareness and out of control. Because of that, planets in those houses can have a hard time expressing themselves in a positive way.

Planets in bad houses averse the Ascendant can also express as working against you in ways that are out of your awareness and control.

In the previous section we considered the houses in terms of angularity and strength of action. Here we have to take into account how house position can also affect the quality of the action of the planet along with its strength and prominence.

Retrograde

In a system that greatly values order and regularity, any planet that is moving against the usual order is suspect, and is a problem. That is what retrograde is - moving against the grain.

Retrogradation traditionally hinders, impedes, slows down, delays, blocks, and weakens. When evaluating the strength of a planet, being retrograde is considered to be a major debility.

Psychologically, a retrograde period can also be a turning attention within, becoming more introverted in its effect. This correlates with a weakening of its outer effectiveness.

A planet in direct motion is considered trustworthy, and a retrograde planet is the opposite, so it could mean not being reliable, or going back on your word, or not being truthful.

Going against the usual order means that a retrograde planet can also express as being rebellious.

If you understand how the planetary motion works, it is possible to spot when a planet is about to change direction by noticing its distance from the Sun in degrees. There is one system for Mercury and Venus, the two planets nearest the Sun, and another for the remaining planets which are further away from the Sun than the Earth.

Outer Planet Retrograde Cycle

The retrograde cycle for the outer planets is pictured here. By 'outer' here I mean all the planets further away from the Sun than the Earth, from Mars on out.

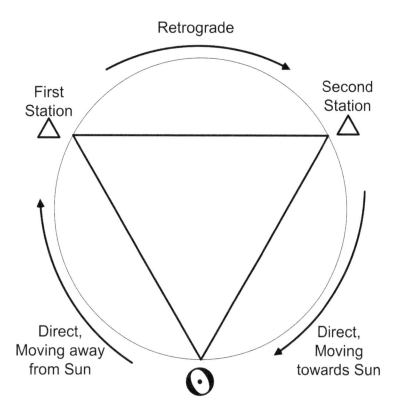

Start the cycle at the bottom of the diagram, as the planet is moving away from conjunction with the Sun. Direction of motion here is clockwise.

Since the Sun moves more quickly than any of the outer planets, the distance between the planet and the Sun is increasing in the left half of this diagram due to the Sun's motion.

When an outer planet is less than approximately 120 degrees from the Sun its motion is direct. Around the 120 degree or trine aspect, the planet slows down and appears to stop, then slowly change direction and move backwards or retrograde.

The point at which the planet appears to stop moving and change direction is called the first station, and it is considered to be very negative. Traditional texts liken it to taking to a sickbed with a serious illness.

For the next 120 degrees of its arc, the planetary motion is retrograde.

As the planet reaches around 120 degrees from the Sun on the other side, it again slows down and stations, and then begins to move direct. This second station is considered to be positive, and is likened to a person getting up from a sickbed after a period of illness.

Past the second station at the trine, the planet gradually picks up speed and goes direct, and continues direct through to its conjunction with the Sun and past. On the right half of this diagram, the Sun is decreasing the distance from the outer planet due to its faster motion. Thus, in that right half of the cycle, the planet is approaching the Sun.

When a planet is stationing, standing still and changing direction, its effect is greatly emphasized and increased for good or ill. This stationary period, when the planet hardly moves at all, is not just a single moment in time, and it gets longer for planets with an orbit further from the Sun. For Saturn, the effective stationary period is around three weeks, and its effect can be felt for a few weeks either side of that. I have noticed an effect with Mars being near a station from as far as three weeks away from exact station. It is important to view the station as a period of some days or weeks rather than a single point in time.

Whenever you see an outer planet that at roughly a trine aspect to the Sun, it is near a station. It is worth picking up an ephemeris and looking for the exact date. The stationing effect can be felt for a couple of weeks on either side of that date, so you can consider any outer planet in an approximate trine aspect to the Sun to have the effects of a station. It is well worth scanning for.

Inner Planet Retrograde Cycle

The two inner planets, Mercury and Venus, never get very far away from the Sun. You can spot whether one of those planets is about to change direction by watching its distance in degrees away from the Sun's position, as in the following diagram.

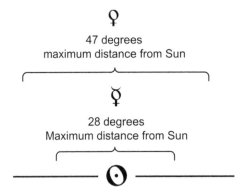

Mercury's maximum distance from the Sun is around 28 degrees, and the maximum distance for Venus is around 47 degrees. When it approaches its maximum distance it slows down and starts to turn around.

For either of these planets, if they are in an earlier degree than the Sun and are direct they are moving towards conjunction with the Sun. In later degrees while direct they are moving away from the Sun.

Each of these planets has its first station, about to turn retrograde, when it is moving direct and approaches its maximum distance in front of the Sun, at a later zodiac degree. Like first station for the outer planets, this is considered negative.

The second station is when it is moving retrograde and reaches its maximum distance behind the Sun, at an earlier zodiac degree. As the planets approach this maximum distance, within a few degrees, they start to slow down, turn around and go direct.

Whenever you see Mercury or Venus near its furthest degree distance from the Sun it will be near a station, and you will have the same intensifying affect for good or ill as with the outer planets. It is worth picking up an ephemeris and checking for the exact date, and you will have an intensified effect for each of these planets for a day or two on either side of the exact turning.

To see if an inner planet is near station, remember that Mercury stations at a little less than one sign away from the Sun. The station happens when Mercury's degree is almost the same as the Sun's degree. Venus stations at a little more than a sign and a half away from the Sun, so take the Sun's degree and either add or subtract 15 degrees. When Venus is in the vicinity of that degree it is near a station.

Combustion

Being conjunct the Sun - either under the Sun's Beam's, or Combust if very close - is said to rob a planet of strength. That makes sense if you think of looking up at the sky. If a planet is anywhere near the Sun, you can't see it, since it is completely overwhelmed by the brightness and hotness of the Sun's fire.

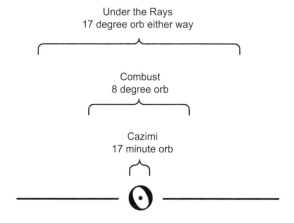

A planet that is peregrine or debilitated will have more of a negative affect from combustion than one which has an essential dignity. In Hellenistic astrology a planet in combustion that is in its rulership is referred to being In its Chariot, and that protects from the negative effects of combustion.

Along with weakening a planet, being in combustion can mean being hidden. Since the planet is literally hidden behind the Sun it can refer to action out of public view. In some situations combustion can mean not being objective. For instance, Mercury very near the Sun could mean that you are not as objective as someone who has Mercury out from under the rays and visible. Mercury in combustion thus could mean that you have no distance from your thinking and you have a hard time being detached and objective. Mercury near the Sun could mean you like to keep secrets.

To show the difference that dignity makes in combustion I want to contrast two charts here. The first is the chart of writer William Burroughs, and the second is the chart of rock star Mick Jagger.

William Burroughs

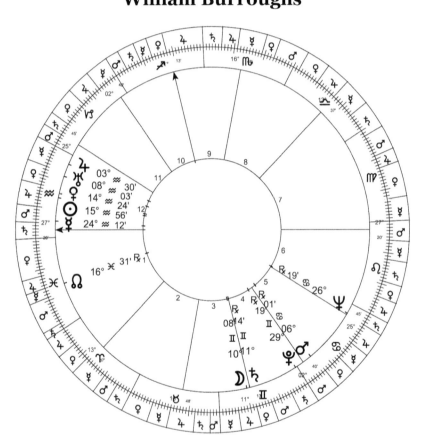

William Seward Burroughs, February 5, 1914, 7:40 AM, St Louis, Missouri. Rodden Rating AA. Placidus house system.

114

	Traditional Full Dignities						
Pl	Ruler	Exalt	Tripl	Term	Face	Detri	Fall
☉	♄	--	♄☿♃	♃	☿	☉ -	--
☽	☿	☊	♄☿♃	♃	♂	♃	--
☿	♄ m	--	♄☿♃ +	♂	☽	☉	--
♀	♄	--	♄☿♃	♃	☿	☉	--
♂	☽	♃	♀♂☽ +	♂ +	♀	♄	♂ -
♃	♄	--	♄☿♃ +	☿	♀	☉	--
♄	☿ m	☊	♄☿♃ +	♃	♂	♃	--
☊	♃	♀	♀♂☽	☿	♃	☿	☿
⊗	☿	☊	♄☿♃	♂	☉	♃	--
As	♄	--	♄☿♃	♄	☽	☉	--
Mc	♃	☋	☉♃♄	♀	☽	☿	--
☋	☿	☿	♀☽♂	♀	♀	♃	♀

In this chart Venus is a little bit more than a degree away from the Sun and is moving towards combustion. Both Venus and the Sun are peregrine, there is no reception between them and both are in the twelfth house. This combustion is pretty much a total loss for Venus, and the Sun is very weak overall.

Mick Jagger

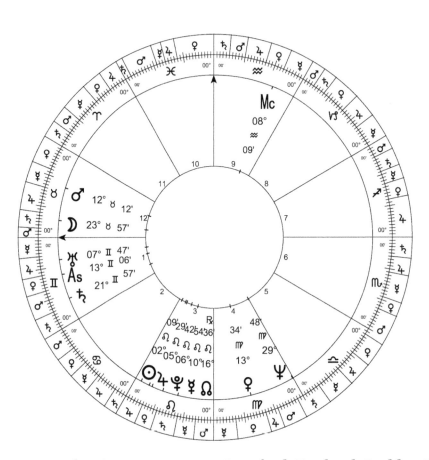

Michael Philip Jagger, July 26, 1943, 2:30 am, Dartford, England. Rodden Rating A. Whole Sign houses.

Pl	Ruler	Exalt	Tripl	Term	Face	Detri	Fall	S
☉	☉ +	--	♃☉♄ +	♃	♄ m	♄	--	-┤
☽	♀	☽ +	☽♀♂ +	♄	♄	♂	--	+
☿	☉	--	♃☉♄	♀	♃	♄	--	
♀	☿	☿	☽♀♂ +	♀ +	♀ +	♃	♀ -	-┤
♂	♀	☽	☽♀♂ +	☿	☽	♂ -	--	
♃	☉	--	♃☉♄ +	♃ +	♄	♄	--	-┤
♄	☿	☊	☿♄♃ +	♂	☉ m	♃	--	+┤
☊	☉	--	♃☉♄	♄	♃	♄	--	
⊗	☉	--	♃☉♄	☿	♂	♄	--	
As	☿	☊	☿♄♃	♀	♂	♃	--	
Mc	♄	--	☿♄♃	♀	♀	☉	--	
☋	♄	--	☿♄♃	♃	☿	☉	--	

By contrast, in Mick Jagger's chart the Sun is applying to conjunction with Jupiter. The Sun has rulership and triplicity, Jupiter has triplicity and term, and each receives the other in multiple minor dignities. Both planets are doing just fine, thank you, which is obvious in the larger than life presence Jagger projects when he walks on stage.

Cazimi

There is another condition called cazimi, being right at the heart of the Sun and greatly strengthened. This happens when the planet is in a very tight orb with the Sun. Most traditional authorities use a 17 minute orb, although I have seen up to a degree orb in some traditional texts.

For an outstanding example of a planet cazimi, see the chapter on the chart of Harry Belafonte in the second part of this book.

Heliacal Rising and Setting

There are two conditions in Hellenistic astrology, called heliacal rising and heliacal setting, when a planet is just about to either emerge from under the rays, or go under the rays. Any planet which will emerge from under the rays within a week of the chart date is making a heliacal rising, coming out from under the Sun's rays and becoming visible again. This is considered to emphasize the planet - like it is waving its planetary hands and saying, *Hi, notice me, I'm back!* Similarly, a planet about to make a heliacal setting is about to go into hiding and loses emphasis.

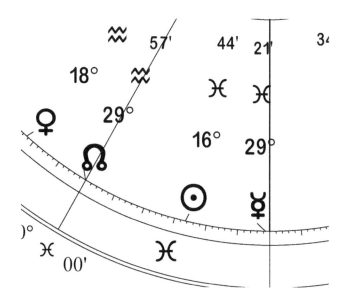

In this diagram, which is from my natal chart, Mercury at 29 Pisces is around 13 degrees from the Sun and will emerge out from under the rays within a week. This means Mercury is making a heliacal rising. Mercury is far more emphasized and important in my chart and life than one would think just by looking at relative dignity and house placement.

The planet Venus in this chart would be considered to be making a heliacal setting if it had been around 26 Aquarius, a couple of degrees more than the 17 degree orb and about to go under the rays.

Oriental and Occidental

Oriental and occidental refers to a planet's position relative to the Sun. A planet is oriental if it rises before the Sun, at an earlier zodiac degree. A planet at a later zodiac degree is called occidental.

The outer planets, Mars, Jupiter and Saturn, are all getting more distant from the Sun when they are oriental, and this strengthens them. For the inner planets, Venus, Mercury and Moon, they are moving away from the Sun when occidental, and this strengthens them.

Being oriental or occidental can affect the quality and expression of the planet. Being oriental, rising before sun, is more public and outward directed, and being occidental, rising after, is less so. For instance, Mercury rising before sun could express as being an orator, a public speaker, while Mercury rising after the Sun is less public, perhaps a writer or someone working behind the scenes.

In the preceding diagram, the Sun is in the third house at 16 Pisces. Mercury is at 29 Pisces and rises after the Sun so it is considered occidental. The planet Venus is at 18 Aquarius, rises before the Sun and is oriental.

Phase of the Moon

In traditional dignity systems, the Moon is considered stronger when it is waxing, increasing in strength. The Moon when it is waning is decreasing in strength, and this is considered a debility.

Of course, phases are also part of a cycle, so in addition to their being related to strength or weakness, there can also be different interpretive meanings for the different phases. As a general rule I have found that the waxing phases are more about doing and creating, waning phases are more about processing and about growth in awareness and learning.

Aspects with other planets

Planets are strengthened or weakened by their aspects with other planets. A planet in hard aspect or conjunct a malefic is considered to be harmed and weakened. A planet in smooth aspect or conjunct a benefic is considered to be benefited and strengthened.

While these are very important interpretive principles, it is also important to recognize that the condition of the planets involved, and the reception between them, are more important than the type of aspect. We will examine this at greater length when we look at how reception affects interpretation.

Besieged

Besieged is a debility condition that happens when a planet is separating from an aspect from one of the malefics, and applying to an aspect from the other malefic. Traditionally this includes only the two planets Saturn and Mars. Some modern astrologers include the three outer planets among the malefics, which means that this condition can happen much more often using the modern criteria.

Besiegement is found in two different ways in traditional texts. In the strictest form it can happen only by conjunction, meaning the besieged planet is physically between the malefics, separating from conjunction to one and applying by conjunction to the other. Besiegement can also happen when applying or separating by one of the other hard aspects, either square or opposition. William Lilly uses only the strict form, and that appears to be the more common usage.

In the strict case of beseigement by conjunction only, if another planet perfects any other aspect to the beseiged planet, by sextile, square, trine or opposition, prior to the conjunction to the second malefic, this is considered to break the seige.

In either of its forms, besiegement is a serious debility - being between a rock and a hard place, going from bad to worse.

Benito Mussolini

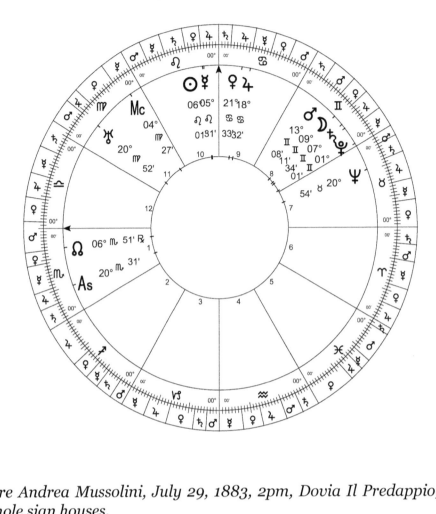

Benito Amilcare Andrea Mussolini, July 29, 1883, 2pm, Dovia Il Predappio, Italy, Rodden Rating AA. Whole sign houses.

In the chart shown here of Italian dictator Benito Mussolini, the Moon is the besieged planet. It is in Gemini in the eighth house, separating from Saturn and applying to Mars, with a tight orb in both cases.

Aided

Aided is the positive flip side to beseigment, where a planet is between aspects to the two benefics, Venus and Jupiter. This is going from good to better. In the strict form it is by conjunction only, in the looser form the aspect can be by trine or sextile. As besiegement is considered to seriously hurt a planet, being aided is considered to seriously help it.

Fixed Stars

Conjunctions with major fixed stars were considered to have an important effect, depending on the nature of the star. The most common way to measure the position of the fixed stars is by ecliptic longitude, a method which has been used for most of the history of Western traditional astrology.

The forward movement of the fixed stars in the zodiac is called Precession. The rate of precession is 1° per 72 years, or 0.838′ per year.

William Lilly considered the following three fixed stars important enough to assign point values in his table of fortitudes and debilities.

The position of the fixed stars given here is for the late twentieth century, approximately 1990. Position is given in terms of zodiacal longitude.

Regulus at 29° 50' Leo - the Royal Star, it signifies honors, power, success, a strong character. It is the star of Kings and leaders of countries when it is auspiciously placed. (Note that Regulus moved into 0 degrees Virgo approximately 2011.)

Spica at 23° 50' Libra - another very positive star, shows fame, honors and good fortune.

Caput Algol at 26° 10' Taurus. Algol or The Ghoul, symbolized by the decapitated head of Medusa, is the most malefic fixed star, and signifies bad fortune, violence, injuries especially involving the head and neck.

If you are interested in working with fixed stars, I recommend the work of Bernadette Brady, which is a good combination of very solid scholarship with both traditional and modern elements of interpretation.

Donald Trump

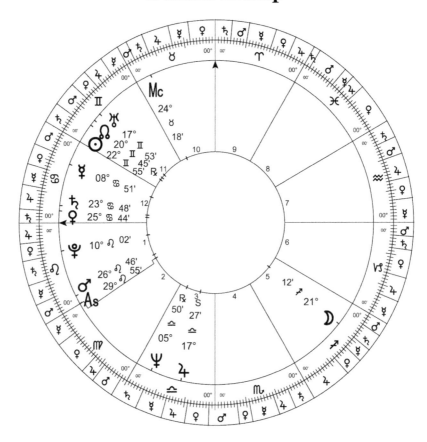

Donald John Trump, June 14, 1946, 10:54 am, Queens, New York. Rodden Rating AA. Whole Sign houses.

The fixed star Regulus is one of the four Persian royal stars. It is one of the brightest of the stars, and one of the closest to the ecliptic, so it is considered very strong. Traditionally Regulus is of the nature of Jupiter and Mars, and is considered very fortunate overall. Having Regulus on an angle is a marker for kings, presidents, and the very wealthy. Regulus is also associated with scandal.

Regulus was very late in the 29th degree of Leo at the time of Donald Trump's birth, very tightly conjunct his Ascendant.

Speed

Planets have an average motion in their daily movement. A planet moving fast is considered to be strengthened. A planet moving slowly is weakened, or doesn't act as quickly.

This is a minor consideration, and I list it here for completeness, since William Lilly includes it in his table of fortitude and debility.

The following table gives the average speed of the planets.

Planet	Average Speed
Moon	13d 10m 36s
Sun	0d 59m 08s
Mercury	0d 59m 08s (same as the Sun)
Venus	0d 59m 08s (same as the Sun)
Mars	0d 31m 27s
Jupiter	0d 4m 59s
Saturn	0d 2m 1s

The Dignities System

As we have seen, the 5 essential dignities did not originate as a single tightly knit system. They were probably each used separately, and then combined in the Hellenistic synthesis. It was not until later in the development of western astrology that the 5 essential dignities were combined into a ranked system.

The combination of essential and accidental dignities are used to show the strength or weakness of a planet and how helpful or harmful its action would be.

Descriptions of the Essential Dignities

By the late Arabic and early European period the descriptions of the different levels of dignity as a system mostly relate to levels of power or responsibility. They are vaguer and less concrete than in the earlier Hellenistic texts.

Here are some quotes from later authors describing the essential dignities.

The Dignities in Ibn Ezra, 11th Century

When a planet is in its domicile, it is like a person in his home.

A planet in its exaltation is like a person at its greatest rank.

A planet in its bound is like a person in his residence or seat.

A planet in its triplicity is like a person with his relatives.

A planet in its face is like a person with fine ornaments and clothing. (p. 135-136)

Note that Ibn Ezra puts bound before triplicity, which was probably the earlier way of ordering those dignities. Also note that triplicity here has the meaning of family relations.

Guido Bonatti, 13th Century

When a planet is in its own domicile, it is like a man who is in his own home...

And while it is in its own exaltation, it is like a man who is in his own kingdom and his own authority, like a kingdom, civil authority, a dukedom...

And while it is in its own term, it is like a man who is among his own kinsmen and blood-relatives and those related by birth, and by kindred, and kin by marriage...

And while it is in its own triplicity, it is like a man who is among his allies and his people, and under officials and followers, who obey him and follow him, who are not related to him out of kinship.

And when it is in its own face, it is like a man who is among unknown people, as sometimes happens to foreigners, and the like, though he lives among them because of an art and profession or service, or because of some other craftsman's or lay art. (Basic p. 73.)

Note in these descriptions that bound or term has taken on the connotation of family, and triplicity is now a wider circle of people who are not blood relations. I think we can view bound or term as immediate family, and triplicity like being extended family or tribe. Bound is more focused and narrow, triplicity is more broad and inclusive.

Also, face here has the meaning of having a place by a profession or a craft, but without any sort of power or authority.

More from Bonatti

Look to see if a malefic planet were the significator of some matter or some beginning, and he were in his domicile or exaltation or bound, or triplicity, and in the angles or succedents: because then he is said to be strong like a benefic.

Note that face is omitted; that any of the other 4 dignities suffices by itself; and that these essential dignities are grouped in with the accidental dignity of angularity by house placement. There is no sharp distinction between essential and accidental dignities, and both are viewed as affecting the strength or weakness of the planet, and the quality of the planet's expression.

William Lilly, 17th Century

When a planet is in his own house, it represents a man in such a condition, as that is Lord of his own house, estate and fortune; or a man wanting very little of the Goods of this world, or it tells you the man is in a very happy state or condition...

If he be in his exaltation, and no way impeded, but Angular; it presents a person of haughty condition, arrogant, assuming more to him than his due...

A planet in his triplicity shows a man modestly endowed with the Goods and Fortune of this world...

A planet fortified, as being only in his own terms, shows a man more of the corporature and temper of the Planet than any extraordinary abundance of fortune, or of eminency in the Commonwealth.

A planet having little or no dignity, but by being in his decanate or face, is almost like a man ready to be turned out of doors, having much ado to maintain himself in credit and reputation...(p. 101-103)

Notice that by the time we reach William Lilly, the different minor dignities have lost pretty much all of their distinct meanings, and have become simple measures of greater or lesser fortune. Lilly makes very little specific use of the minor dignities in his chart interpretation

examples.
Weighing and Combining

Originally there was no clear sense or practice of any of the dignities being stronger than the others. Early texts refer to "rulership or triplicity or exaltation or term" without distinguishing relative strength. It was during the Persian and Arabic periods of traditional astrology that the different dignities were assigned different levels of strength in a ranked system.

Relative Weighting

This is the most common method of weighting the relative strength of the different dignities. It became the standard in English speaking astrology after the publication of William Lilly's Christian Astrology in 1647.

Dignity	Score
Rulership	5
Exaltation	4
Triplicity	3
Term	2
Face	1

In this system of the dignities, triplicity is ranked above bound or term in strength. Lilly used only a single triplicity ruler

There is an alternate method of weighting the 5 dignities, that is likely earlier than the one above, and that appears in Al-Biruni and other authors. Bonatti was aware of both systems and talked of situations in which on or the other would be used.

Dignity	Score
Rulership	5
Exaltation	4
Term	3
Triplicity	2
Face	1

In this system of using the dignities, term or bound is ranked above triplicity.

I prefer this system of ranking, partly because I think term is more important than triplicity, and partly because I use all three triplicity rulers, so it makes sense to give each of them a lower value.

We need a working framework with both the essential and accidental dignities to use for evaluating the condition of any planet point. We will be using the system of scoring fortitudes and debilities from Lilly's *Christian Astrology*. I call this system,

William Lilly's Cheate Sheete

The full cheate sheete appears on the next page, and again at the end of the book.

William Lilly's Cheate Sheete

A ready table whereby to examine the *fortitudes* and *debilities* of the Planets

ESSENTIAL DIGNITIES	RATING	ESSENTIAL DEBILITIES	RATING
Rulership (Domicile)	5	Detriment	-5
Exaltation	4	Fall	-4
Triplicity	3		
Term	2	Peregrine	-5
Face	1		
Rulership and Exaltation are considered MAJOR; Triplicity, Term and Face are considered MINOR.			
Mutual Reception			
by Rulership	5		
by Exaltation	4		
etc			

ACCIDENTAL DIGNITIES		ACCIDENTAL DEBILITIES	
Relative House Strength		**Relative House Strength**	
In MC or ASC	5	In 12th house	-5
In 7th 4th or 11th house	4	In 8th or 6th houses	-4
In 2nd or 5th house	3	*(note: these houses do not*	
In 9th house	2	*aspect or behold the ASC.)*	
In 3rd house	1		
Direct in motion (not ☉ or ☽)	4	Retrograde	-5
Swift in motion	2	Slow in motion	-2
Important Aspects		**Important Aspects**	
partile ☌ ♃ or ♀	5	partile ☌ ♄ or ♂	-5
partile ☌ ☊	4	partile ☌ ☋	-4
partile △ ♃ or ♀	4	partile △ ♄ or ♂	-4
partile ✶ ♃ or ♀	3	partile ✶ ♄ or ♂	-3
Beseiged by ♃ or ♀	5	Beseiged by ♄ or ♂	-5
Free from combustion or sunbeams	5	Combust (8° orb)	-5
Cazimi (heart of ☉)	5	Under the sunbeams (17°)	-4
☽ Occidental (increasing)	2	☽ Oriental (decreasing)	-2
♄ ♃ ♂ oriental	2	♄ ♃ ♂ occidental	-2
♀ ☿ occidental	2	♀ ☿ oriental	-2
☌ Regulus (29 ♌)	6	☌ Caput Algol (26 ♉)	-5
☌ Spica (23 ♎)	5		

Before we go any further I want to strongly emphasize an important point about using this scoring system.

Please don't get too hung up on the points and scoring. While I think they are useful, the primary utility of this system is to train you what to scan for when you look at a chart. Think of going through this scoring system as being like using a set of training wheels when you are learning to ride a bicycle.

This system is not new to Lilly. These conditions are in the writings of the main Arabic astrologers like Sahl and Masha'Allah, and were also collected by Bonatti in his compilation work, *The Book of Astronomy*, into lists of conditions that either help or hinder a planet.

In Lilly's Cheate Sheete we have these conditions arranged in the form of a checklist of positive or negative conditions, each of which is assigned a point value. This will give you a list of positive and negative scores, that you can then total up to get an idea of the overall condition of the planet, how helpful or harmful it is likely to be.

Use this Cheate Sheet checklist and I promise you that you will never look at a chart the same way again. You will have trained yourself to notice the most important features in a planet's condition, and how to weigh and combine them.

Lilly himself used his scoring table primarily as a teaching tool. Book Two of *Christian Astrology* has something like 40 chart examples, and Lilly goes through the scoring system with just one of them. He explains, *"I do this more willingly that young Learners may better understand the use of these Tables, which they will frequently have occasion to use."(p 178)*

Cheate Sheete Sections

Here is a brief overview of the Cheate Sheete.

In the first section we have the scoring for the 5 essential dignities. Points are also given for mutual reception between planets, with the same relative scoring as in stand-alone dignity.

The latter half of the Cheate Sheete covers the different kinds of accidental dignities, that are based on conditions other than zodiacal degree.

The first section of this lower half evaluates strength based on house placement. The angular houses get the highest scores. Note that 3 of the houses that are averse the Ascendant, houses 6, 8 and 12, all get negative scores. This reflects how they weaken planets located there, and also reflects how they can have a negative impact on the quality of the planet.

Next, planets are given scores for being direct or retrograde, or being fast or slow in motion.

The next section covers the effect of aspects. A positive aspect from the benefics or the North Node helps a planet, and a negative aspect from the malefics or the South Node hurts a planet. Lilly uses an orb of a single degree to apply this scoring, but scanning for these will pick up all major aspects with a larger orb.

The bottom section covers miscellaneous conditions. There is combustion or lack thereof, and there is the placement of the planet before or after the Sun. Phase of the Moon is scored with increasing being positive, and decreasing being negative.

Finally, Lilly gives positive or negative scores based on proximity to a few very important fixed stars - Regulus and Spica being positive, and Algol being negative. Lilly uses a pretty generous orb for some fixed stars, depending on their magnitude and their closeness to the ecliptic. For these three fixed stars he uses up to a 5 or 6 degree orb.

For our purposes here I have a slightly revised system of scoring the dignities and debilities. This is a new and improved system, which I have named,

Charlie's Cheate Sheete

The full cheate sheete appears on the next page, and again at the end of the book.

Here are the points where I have adjusted the scoring based on my experience. You will most likely come up with your own adjustments after you have mastered the system.

Triplicity and Term - Lilly gives the single triplicity ruler 3 points and the term ruler 2 points. I go with an alternate tradition and give the term ruler 3 points, and give each of the three triplicity rulers 2 points.

Peregrine - Lilly gives a peregrine planet -5; I reduce it to -3. I think it does deserve a minus score, but I do not think it is as negative as a major debility. Peregrine planets are very strongly affected by the location and condition of their ruling planets, so take that into account. If an otherwise peregrine planet has major mutual reception or its equivalent that could be considered to take away the planet's peregrine status.

Sect - Recent work on traditional astrology has recovered how important sect is in chart interpretation. To reflect this, I give planets in the sect of a chart a +3 score, and planets out of sect, a -3 score.

Antiscia / Contrantiscia - Aspects by Antiscia or Contrantiscia, within about a 2 degree orb, can be very strong. Give planets in Antiscia to Jupiter or Venus a +5. Give planets in Antiscia OR Contrantiscia to Mars or Saturn a -5.

Heliacal Rising / Setting - A planet that is about to emerge from under the Sun's rays within a week is said to be making a Heliacal Rising. It increases the planet's prominence, and I assign it a +5. The reverse, a planet that is moving into the Sun's rays within a week, is said to be making a Heliacal setting. This greatly weakens the planet, and I assign it a -5. This overrides the condition of combustion or being under the rays. It helps you to realize the great difference between moving towards the Sun and moving away. *Note that I use heliacal rising instead of the negative score for being under the rays, and I use heliacal setting instead of the positive score for not being combust.*

Charlie's Cheate Sheete

A new, improved table whereby to examine the fortitudes and debilities of the Planets

ESSENTIAL DIGNITIES	RATING	ESSENTIAL DEBILITIES	RATING
Rulership (Domicile)	5	Detriment	-5
Exaltation	4	Fall	-4
Term	3		
Triplicity	2	Peregrine	-3
Face	1		
Mutual Reception			
by Rulership	5		
by Exaltation	4		
(etc - include major mixed receptions)			
In Sect	3	Out of Sect	-3

ACCIDENTAL DIGNITIES		ACCIDENTAL DEBILITIES	
Relative House Strength		**Relative House Strength**	
In MC or ASC	5	In 12th house	-5
In 7th 4th or 11th house	4	In 8th or 6th houses	-4
In 2nd or 5th house	3	*(note: these houses do not*	
In 9th house	2	*aspect or behold the ASC.)*	
In 3rd house	1		
Direct in motion (not ☉ or ☽)	4	Retrograde	-5
Swift in motion	2	Slow in motion	-2
Important Aspects		**Important Aspects**	
close ☌ ♃ or ♀	5	close ☌ ♄ or ♂	-5
close ☌ ☊	4	close ☌ ☋	-4
close △ ♃ or ♀	4	close ☍ ♄ or ♂	-4
close ✳ ♃ or ♀	3	close □ ♄ or ♂	-3
(2° applying, 1° separating)			
Beseiged by ♃ or ♀	5	Beseiged by ♄ or ♂	-5
Antiscia to ♃ or ♀	5	Antiscia or Contrantiscia to ♄ or ♂	-5
Free from combustion or sunbeams	5	Combust (7° orb)	-5
Cazimi (heart of ☉)	5	Under the sunbeams (17°)	-4
Heliacal Rising	5	Heliacal Setting	-5
☽ Occidental (increasing)	2	☽ Oriental (decreasing)	-2
♄ ♃ ♂ oriental	2	♄ ♃ ♂ occidental	-2
♀ ☿ occidental	2	♀ ☿ oriental	-2
☌ Regulus (29 ♌) 6° orb	6	☌ Caput Algol (26 ♉) 6° orb	-5
☌ Spica (23 ♎) 6° orb	5		

Terms of a Benefic or Malefic - It is common for traditional texts to view a planet in the bounds of a benefic as strengthened, and a planet in the bounds of a malefic as weakened. To reflect that, I give a +2 for being in the bounds of a benefic, and a -2 for being in the bounds of a malefic. (This is a minor condition.)

To illustrate how this scoring system is used, here is a sample chart from William Lilly, showing how to evaluate some of the main planets in the chart.

Example - If He Be Rich or Poor

This chart is from Lilly, p. 177. It is the only chart in the horary volume where he walks through adding up the dignities and debilities from his table, to show how to use it.

This is the same chart data as it appears in *Christian Astrology*, but it is drawn in modern format. I have hand drawn this chart, giving all of the planets and houses the exact degree positions that Lilly used. Re-casting the chart with a modern software program often changes some of the positions. Note that, for any examples from Lilly, I use his system of triplicity and term rulers to be consistent with his practice, and I use his version of the scoring system.

If He be Rich or Poor

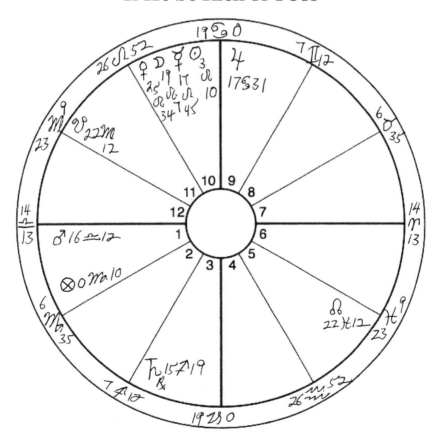

Here are examples from Lilly of weighing up a planet in this chart.

Mars His Dignities	His Debilities
No essential dignities	In detriment -5
In the Asc +5	Peregrine -5
Direct motion +4	Occidental of Sun -2
Not combust +5	
Conjunct fixed star Spica +5	
Total +21	Total -12

Combined total for Mars: +9

In Lilly's judgment, Mars is basically a positive influence in the chart. Even though Mars is peregrine and in detriment, Lilly judges the planet to be helpful based on the preponderance of positive dignities overall.

Jupiter His Fortitudes	
In Exaltation, +4	*He has no Debilities, either accidental or Essential, yet some Detriment it is to him, being in Square with Mars, though the aspect be platic (not in the same degree).*
In the 10th +5	
Direct motion +4	
Not combust +5	
Swift motion +2	
Total +20	

Total for Jupiter: +20

As Lilly points out, the square to Mars is not counted in the scoring since it is not within a degree orb, but he does note it as having a detrimental effect.

Saturn His Dignities	His Debilities
No essential dignities	Peregrine -5
In the 3rd House +1	Retrograde -5
Not combust +5	Slow in motion -2
	Occidental of Sun -2
Total +6	Total -14

Combined total for Saturn: -8

Saturn is the most debilitated planet in the chart.

After going through each of the other planets in turn, Lilly begins his overall judgment with this summary statement.

Herein first I considered the general disposition of the Planets, and found that the Major number of them (especially the two Fortunes) were swift in their motion, well placed in houses, no manner of ways in a violent way, or by a forcible aspect afflicting each other.

Because the majority of the planets are in good shape, Lilly gives a positive judgment to this chart. Rather than dwelling on individual dignities or debilities, he uses the overall condition for his conclusion.

Using the Dignities

Essential Dignities and General Chart Evaluation

This is a series of steps to use to gather the useful information about dignity from a chart. Throughout this process you are looking for planets that stand out, and you are looking for significant patterns, especially repeating patterns.

1) Start with Sect

Start with noting the sect of the chart, and look at the locations of the planets in sect and out of sect. Other things being equal, the benefic of the sect of the chart will be the most beneficial planet, and the malefic out of sect will be the source of most difficulty. Note location of these planets and the houses they rule to identify their areas.

2) Check Essential Dignity Next

Look for the major dignities and debilities - rulership and detriment, exaltation and fall.

After the preliminary scan of the major dignities, look at all five of the essential dignities. Scan to see if any planets dominate in any way. Planets with major essential dignity or debility are likely to be important. Include planets with two or more minor dignities as being equivalent to a major dignity. Also consider overall predominance of any one planet in essential dignities overall, or in a single one of the dignities, as we noticed with Mercury in bounds in the chart of Maya Angelou.

3) Weigh up Essential and Accidental (the Cheate Sheete checklist)

Once you have essential dignity, look at accidental dignity for how prominent the planet will be and how much of an opportunity it will get to act. This is the step where I add up the points. Once you have the scores, then list the planets in order from highest to lowest to get an idea of which are likely the most helpful, and the most harmful. Planets that are either very strong or very weak are likely to be featured in some way.

4) Look for Major Mutual Receptions

Check for mutual receptions, especially in major dignities. On the first main scan I look at just major mutual receptions - ruler to ruler, exalted to exalted, ruler to exalted. I bring in the minor dignities when I am looking at a particular planet or point in detail.

Without exception I find that major mutual reception plays a dominant part in how the chart plays out.

5) Check for Final Dispositor

Check for a final dispositor, including a pair of final dispositors in mutual reception. That planet or planets will likely be an organizing point for the whole chart.

6) Check the Angles

Look at the rulers of the Ascendant and Midheaven - see which planet(s) dominate the angles. Also consider the condition of any planets near the angles as they are likely to be visible and prominent.

7) Evaluate Major Aspects and Aspect Patterns

Check for aspects and aspect patterns. With each major aspect, always check the reception of the planets involved. This will tell which of the planets will dominate, and how they receive each other's actions.

Throughout this process you have gathered a lot of information about the planets, and the next step is to check for the patterns of the chart, the elements that tie it together.

What Stands Out

Throughout this process you are looking for the standout features of the chart. That will likely include one of more of these configurations.

- particularly strong or weak planets
- houses with 2 or more planets
- angular planets (especially at the Ascendant and Midheaven) and their condition
- a final dispositor or mutual co-dispositors
- any particularly strong aspects or aspect patterns
- planet or planets dominating in overall dignities, especially at the angles or with angular planets
- any strong repeating theme

By the time you are done with scanning the items I listed above, you should be ready to take parts of the chart that seem important to you, and put them under a microscope. This is where you go into detail of looking at all the major and minor dignities, the details of reception, and so on.

Now we are ready to take the system of dignities and focus it on a single house.

Dignity for Evaluating a House

Evaluating a specific house topic involves the same condition.

First, consider any planets in the house, what condition are they in, what houses they rule, if they see the houses they rule, and what aspects they make to other planets. House topics are linked by rulerships and by aspects.

With the sign at house cusp, consider the domicile, exaltation and triplicity rulers as affecting the entire house. (You can look at term and face rulers for all houses, but I tend to use them only on the four angles.) You ask exactly the same questions of these rulers that you do of any other planets in the chart.

For a single house you now have several influences to consider, some quite strong, some weak, some positive, some negative. Look for what predominates, weigh up the strengths and weaknesses and judge accordingly.

Herman Melville

This is an exercise in evaluating the tenth house of career and reputation in the chart of classic writer Herman Melville.

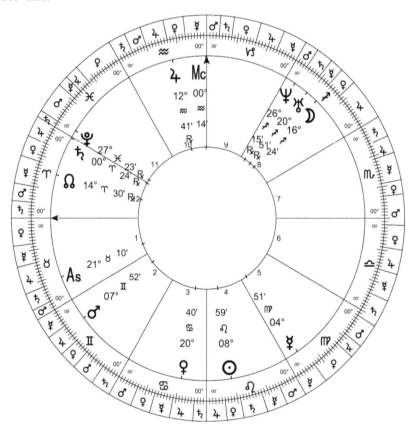

Herman Melville, August 1, 1819, 11:30 PM, New York, New York. Rodden Rating AA. Whole Sign houses.

The tenth house ruler is Saturn, in fall in the twelfth house. Jupiter is in the 10th house with dignity by triplicity and should be helpful.

Mercury also has dignity at the Midheaven by triplicity but is averse the Ascendant, which weakens its effect on the MC. The Midheaven is in the terms of Mars, and we noticed earlier that Mercury dominates Mars and they work well together. Earlier we noted how Melville's sea writings have a combined Mercury Mars flavor.

The combination of Jupiter and Saturn is seen in the mix of good and bad fortune that Melville had with his writing. With Saturn in the twelfth, Melville was convinced his publishers were his enemies and were secretly working against him.

Traditionally a planet in a house determines the beginning fortune of that house topic, and the ruler of the house determines the later development and end of the matter. In Melville's case this is Jupiter for the beginning, and Saturn for the ending. Melville's first two books were adventure novels of his sea travels, and were popular best-sellers. His later, more serious work was poorly received, and he was not able to find a publisher for his late work. Melville ended his life unhappy and in obscurity.

Dignities and the Outer Planets

The outer planets do not have any essential dignity in the traditional sense. The traditional rulers are responsible for implementing its effect, and the ruler with the most dignities will likely have the main responsibility. Take these rulers into account with outer planets in aspect.

If you find any of the three modern outer planets at an angle, look carefully at its dignities, to see which planets are ruling it since they will be responsible for dealing with the effects of that outer planet. The outer planets always have to work through the inner planets to affect our lives.

Bob Dylan

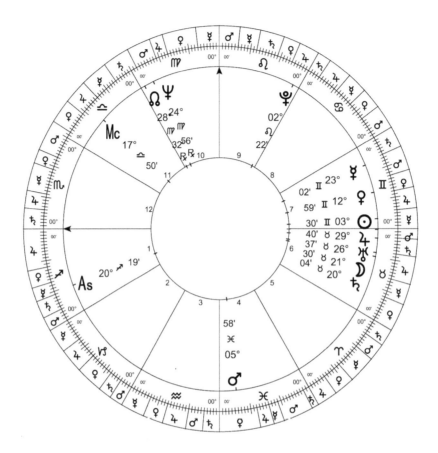

Robert Allen Zimmerman, May 24, 1941, 9:05 PM, Duluth, Minnesota. Rodden Rating AA. Whole Sign houses.

In Bob Dylan's chart, note that Neptune is in the 10th house in Virgo. It is conjunct the North Node, which should tend to magnify its effect. Neptune is ruled by Mercury in his rulership in Gemini, and the two planets make a tight square.

I think the Neptune influence is very visible in Dylan's songwriting, especially his wilder material from the sixties. The Neptune effect then was amplified by the fact that Dylan was a pretty heavy drug user during this period.

Backup Plan

This is a common procedure in many traditional texts. For a given planet or point, go through the rulers in order until you find one that is in good condition. Start with the sign ruler, and if that planet is in bad condition, look at the exalted ruler, and so on down the chain of all the dignities. The ruler that is in the best overall condition will likely be the most influential.

The backup plan is especially important when you have a planet that is debilitated, and also with all peregrine planets. Having one of its rulers in good shape and aspecting it can help a lot with how the planet expresses.

Charles Obert

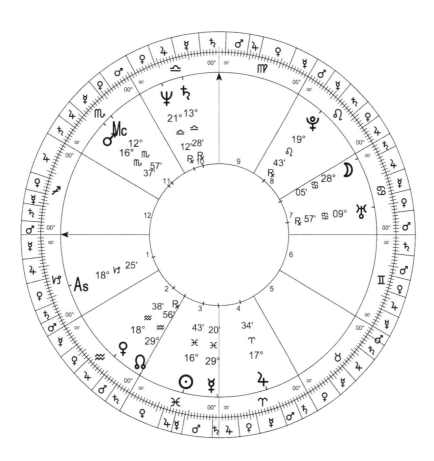

In my natal chart shown here, Mercury is peregrine and in detriment and in fall in the last degree of Pisces - very unstable! The house ruler Jupiter is averse, and so is the exalted ruler Venus, so neither offers immediate support. The Moon is one of the triplicity rulers of Mercury and is strong and angular, in rulership, triplicity and face. Mars is another triplicity ruler for Mercury and is also angular and strong in its in rulership and triplicity. Both the Moon and Mars strongly affect how Mercury expresses in my life. There is a strong emotional and intuitional component to my thinking and writing, and I have a very strong, Mars in Scorpio think-for-yourself streak to my personality.

Linking Houses

This principle is very simple, and you will see it very widely used in traditional chart interpretation. Linking the topics of houses by their common rulers is one of the most important ways to use the dignity system, and it appears repeatedly in traditional texts. Morin makes linking houses by rulership one of the keystones of his interpretive system.

There are three main ways that the linking of houses and house topics should be used.

Houses Ruled by One Planet

The first, and most primary, concerns a planet and the houses it rules. There is a connection between the house a planet occupies and the houses where it has rulership.

1) If you have a dominant planet, its location and the houses it rules will likely be important for the person, and their themes will likely be connected.

Donald Trump

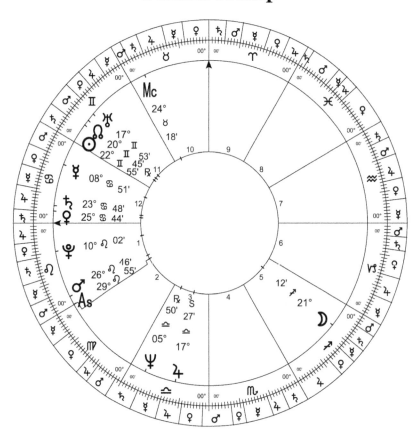

Donald John Trump, June 14, 1946, 10:54 AM, Queens, New York. Rodden Rating AA. Whole Sign houses.

Jupiter is making a trine to the Sun that is 5 degrees past exact. If you check an ephemeris, Jupiter is just a few hours from its exact second station. Jupiter also has dignity by both triplicity and term, so it is strong by essential dignity and further strengthened by being at station.

Jupiter rules the fifth and eighth houses. Connecting them here, we get gambling and games of chance (fifth house) connected with other people's money (eighth house) - in other words, casinos.

We also used this principle of linking houses with their ruler when we looked at sect. The benefic matching the sect of the chart is a likely source of good fortune, and you look to the location of the planet, and the houses the planet rules, to see where that good fortune will originate, and where it can most likely manifest.

Houses of Planets in Mutual Reception

Mutual reception between planets also links the houses occupied by the planets. Since major mutual reception is important this means that, if you have two planets in a major mutual reception, the houses they each occupy will likely be important areas of focus for the person - look at ways the house meanings can combine in their expression. Just as the mutual reception serves as a main organizing principle for the chart, the house topics are part of that organizing principle.

When we look at the chart of Pope Francis in the second part of the book, you will see that houses connected by a major mutual reception are the core of his chart.

Houses of Planets in Aspect

This is one technique for connecting houses that is widely used in modern astrology also. House location and topics need to be considered with any planets in major aspect. As in the previous examples of connection, you need to evaluate the quality of the planets, their mutual reception or lack thereof, to see if those house areas of life will work together or will conflict.

For instance, if you have a square between planets in the seventh and tenth houses this could play out as a conflict between relationships and career - the person finds these two parts of their lives in tension and needs to choose between them.

On Combining House Meanings

As Morin points out, the linking between the house topics will vary, and will depend on the affinity of meanings between the two houses.

For instance, if there is a link by rulership between the sixth and eighth houses this does not mean that all of your pets will die.

Similarly, how the houses link will vary from person to person. In Trump's chart we saw the link between the fifth and eighth houses as relating to his casinos, games of chance and entertainment with other people's money. In another chart, depending on the condition of the planets and other factors, that same fifth and eighth houses could play out as the death of a child.

For that reason, I think we really need to get information about the life context of the people whose charts we interpret, in order to take houses with multiple meanings and know how the house connection plays out in their individual lives. I think that astrology can determine and predict categories and areas and not specifics.

The second half of this book is a series of chart examples. Their purpose is to show how the evaluation of dignity, debility and reception is central to interpretation.

Extended Chart Examples

Clara Barton

Clara Barton is best known as the founder of the American Red Cross, and she did extensive work in field hospitals during the Civil War. Barton also contributed to public education and was a major spokesperson for the women's suffrage movement.

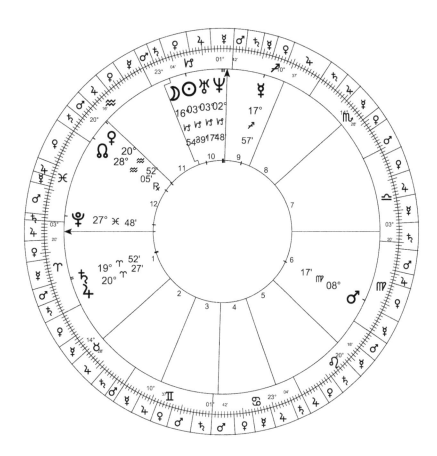

Clara Barton, December 25, 1821, 11:52 AM, Oxford, Massachusetts. Rodden Rating B. Placidus Houses.

We will focus on the core planets that show her vocation.

Mars is the Lord of her rising sign, Aries. The Lord of the first house represents the person and Mars is in the sixth house of nursing. She was born to be a nurse, it is her identity and vocation. Mars in the sixth house is also associated with the military, and much of her nursing work was done during the Civil War with the troops.

Mars has dignity by triplicity. Triplicity is about being part of a larger group. Mars in triplicity is her working with the army doing nursing on the battlefields. The soldiers she worked with recognized her as one of them, on their side. The soldiers were her tribe, her triplicity.

Mars and Venus have mutual reception by term, and Venus is in the twelfth house, which is associated with self-sacrifice, and large institutions like hospitals and nursing homes.

Planets that are in mutual reception have a mutually supportive role, they are each pledged to help the other. It shows a strong supportive bond. Both the sixth and twelfth houses are associated with nursing, and here with mutual reception by terms the planets work together at a practical level.

Saturn is the rising planet in this chart and is in its fall in Aries, but with dignity by triplicity. A planet in fall is one that is not respected or given the credit it deserves. This correlates to a consistent pattern in Clara Barton's life. Repeatedly, she worked to build a service organization like a school or a hospital. When it became large and successful the powers that be took the organization away from her and gave it to men at a much higher pay rate.

A planet in fall can also be an advocate and spokesperson for a community in fall, a group of people who are not respected or given the dignity they deserve. Clara Barton was a major spokesperson in the Women's Suffrage movement, speaking for women who as a group were in fall, without respect or power.

Saturn is trine to Mercury in Aquarius in the ninth house of travel and teaching. Mercury is in detriment, but has dignity by triplicity and term. Again we see dignity in triplicity and term as getting work done in a team. Mercury in detriment is Barton as a woman and second class citizen. Mercury is strong in some ways and weak in others, expressing her role as a women's suffrage spokesperson.

How Canterbury Would Die

This chart is from William Lilly's masterpiece, *Christian Astrology*. It is a good example of using dignity, and it is also a lovely example of multiple complementary pointers to the same answer.

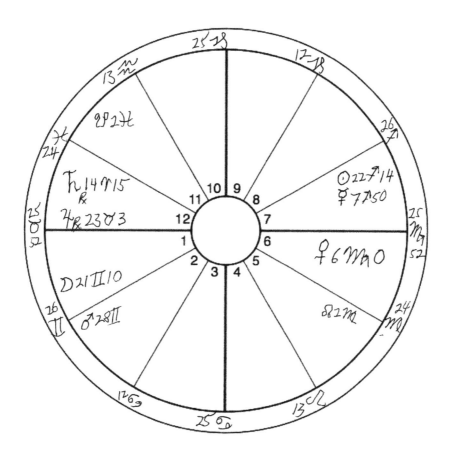

I drew this chart by hand to give the planet positions and house cusps at exactly the same location Lilly used. If you run this chart with modern astrology software there is a discrepancy in planet and house locations.

The question being asked here is, **By what manner of death Canterbury shall die?** Canterbury here is the Archbishop of Canterbury, head of the Church of England. At the time Lilly cast the chart the Archbishop was fallen from power and in prison. The question was not, Will he die, but How.

"It may appear to all indifferent minded men [indifferent here meaning impartial, unbiased], the verity & worth of Astrologie by this Question, for there is not any amongst the wisest of men in this world could better have represented the person and condition of this old man his present state and condition, and the manner of his death, then this present figure of heaven doth."

This is a question about a church leader, so we look to the ninth house and its lord Saturn, in fall and retrograde in the twelfth house in the intercepted sign Aries. The twelfth house connotes imprisonment and loss of power and status. A planet in fall is in disgrace and fallen. Some traditional texts translate the word for fall as prison.

Lilly mentions that Jupiter is a general Significator of churchmen and 'doth somewhat also represent his condition'. That will become important a bit later on.

Lilly's main analysis focuses on the Moon who is lord of the fourth house of endings. The fourth house is also the derived eighth house from the ninth house of the question, the house of a church related death. The Moon is applying to an opposition to the Sun which is on the cusp of the eighth house of death, and the Sun in turn is applying to an opposition with Mars. Mars is important here as the ruler of Saturn in Aries, representing the person who controls the archbishop.

"Mars being in an Airy Signe and humane, from hence I judged that he should not be hanged, but suffere a more noble kind of death... He was beheaded."

Lilly had judged a humane form of death since Mars was in a human air sign. This inclines Mars to give the archbishop a "more noble" kind of death.

There is another very striking marker for beheading here - **Saturn itself in its fall is in Aries which signifies the head - his head fell off**.

I use this chart in a class I teach on dignities at Kepler College. Jupiter is conjunct the Ascendant at 24 Taurus, peregrine and retrograde and in the twelfth house. One of the participants pointed out that Jupiter is conjunct the fixed star Algol. **Algol, literally The Ghoul, is a very malefic star associated with the decapitated head of Medusa,** signifying beheading.

Lilly also notes Jupiter is natural significator of religion and the church. Jupiter being conjunct the Ascendant, it is worth our looking at the Ascendant Lord.

Taurus is rising so the lord is Venus in the sixth house in detriment and peregrine. A debilitated Venus also represents the Archbishop in prison. Venus is moving towards the descendant which is in opposition to the Ascendant and thus associated with ending of life.

The only aspect Venus makes is an opposition to Jupiter, and **Jupiter is lord of the eighth house of death and of the twelfth house of prisons and confinement - death in prison**. The lord of the first house applying to lord of the eighth is a classic marker for death. With Jupiter retrograde this is a mutual application, meaning the two planets are approaching each other. This indicates an abrupt and negative conclusion.

In the opposition from Jupiter to Venus there is no reception from Jupiter - Jupiter has no dignity where Venus is - and that is a further marker for the opposition being negative in effect. Venus receives Jupiter into her house, and some traditional texts state that Lord of the first receiving Lord of the eighth is a sure marker for death since The lord of death is welcomed in and can do what he will.

Jupiter, Lord of the eighth house of death is also conjunct the Ascendant itself - yet another marker for death.

More precisely, **Jupiter is in Taurus which is associated with the neck - death by having his neck cut**. Jupiter is a benefic even when debilitated, which is associated with the relatively humane form of death.

Jupiter here as signifying both the church and the killing planet has another literal and apt meaning. Canterbury was killed by Presbyterian church reformers in England who felt that Canterbury's form of the Church of England needed to be destroyed. **Jupiter here really is both the church and the killing planet - Canterbury was killed by the Church**.

In each of these instances the symbolism is striking and apt. We saw the same meaning whether we used the Lord of the ninth house (Saturn) or the natural ruler of the church (Jupiter) or the lord of the Ascendant (Venus). It is also a good example of taking the chart symbolism concretely and literally.

Harry Belafonte

I discovered the music of Harry Belafonte when I was in college in the early 1970's, at the start of the hard rock era. Along with his artistry I deeply admire the man's dedication to his principles and his work as an outspoken civil rights activist. He is that rare sort of person who lives a life consistent with his principles, with a moral integrity that gives his words and actions power and influence.

Belafonte's chart is very beautiful. It has a symmetry and interconnectedness that is aesthetically pleasing.

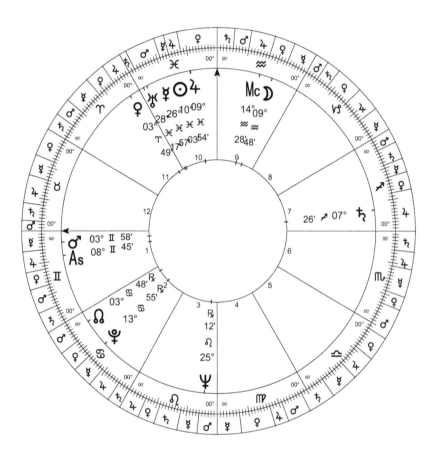

Harry Belafonte, March 1, 1927, 10:30 AM, New York, New York. Rodden Rating AA.

All seven of the traditional planets, plus Uranus, are above the horizon - a clear marker for a publicly visible career.

Jupiter

The outstanding planet in this chart is Jupiter, in rulership in Pisces in the 10th house. Jupiter is also **conjunct the Sun within 8 minutes of arc**. This is **cazimi**, being at the heart of the Sun, and it is one of the strongest and most positive conditions for a planet.

148

Jupiter is also final dispositor of the chart.

Jupiter rules the tenth house it is in, and the seventh house. The tenth house is career and reputation, so this is an obvious marker for a highly successful public life.

Belafonte was married three times, and the second marriage to dancer Julie Robertson lasted 50 years. He was married a third time in 2008. (Saturn on the Descendant could point to him as an older man marrying a younger woman.) A mutable sign on the seventh house points to the possibility of multiple marriages, and the ruler Jupiter points to their being good quality and successful.

Mars

Mars sits prominently on the Ascendant, and Mars is peregrine and is out of sect. I think that peregrine Mars manifests as his being an outspoken civil rights activist. Belafonte was good friends and co-workers with Martin Luther King.

Mars rules the sixth house (servants and slaves) and the eleventh houses (friends and community). Belafonte spent much of his early childhood in Jamaica, and he identified with the black laborers and slaves in Jamaica. He also spent time in an English boarding school, so he learned first hand what it was like to have a darker skin than your superiors. This is a life-long identification and the core of his identity. His most famous song, The Banana Boat Song (*Day-O*) is about the poor blacks working on banana plantations in Jamaica.

Since Mars rules both the sixth and the eleventh houses those two areas of his life are connected. Belafonte's chosen friends and his community are poor oppressed blacks. I think that this community identification led him to turn to folk rather than popular songs for the heart of his musical repertoire. Folks songs are the songs of the poor and working class, not popular society music.

  In 2001 Belafonte released a major anthology titled, *The Long Road to Freedom: An Anthology of Black Music*. That work sums up the connection between his music, his chosen community, and his social activist idealism.

Mercury

As the Lord of the Ascendant, we look to Mercury to see how Belafonte presents himself to the world, along with that prominent Mars conjunct the Ascendant.

Mercury is the most debilitated planet in the chart, in detriment and fall in Pisces in the 10th house. Looking at the dignities of Mercury, Mars has dignity with Mercury by triplicity and term and face, while Mercury rules Mars. This gives the two planets the equivalent of major mutual reception. In addition, Mercury is in a very tight applying sextile with Mars which is within two minutes of being exact, so we should expect Mercury and Mars to work tightly together.

Notice also that Mercury is in an applying conjunction with Uranus, within less than two degrees of exact. That emphasizes the same qualities of being independent and outspoken.

Mercury joining with Mars here represents Belafonte as civil rights activist and spokesman. Mars being peregrine and Mercury in detriment and fall are mirrored in Belafonte being a member of, and spokesperson for, an out group with no respect and no power. It also likely means that his speech is not always controlled, and it can have a sharp Mars edge to it. With Mercury linked to both Mars and Uranus, Belafonte could be very brash and outspoken, and did not hesitate to stand alone and speak the truth even when it was unwelcome or dangerous.

He publicly criticized Condoleeza Rice while she was secretary of state, and also famously criticized President Obama as "lacking a moral compass" and said he didn't deserve a second term. When Obama asked Belafonte why he didn't cut Obama any slack, Belafonte answered, *"What makes you think we haven't?"* That is the voice of the Mars/Mercury combination.

Mercury is 16 degrees from the Sun and moving direct, so he is making a heliacal rising and coming out from under the Sun, which emphasizes his importance. Heliacal rising here is a good metaphor for Belafonte emerging from out of obscurity and poverty, and is also reflected in his activism, acting spokesmen for the oppressed, making visible a group that was obscured before.

We have two important sides of Belafonte the man here - the Mars/Mercury combination as the civil rights activist, and the Sun/Jupiter combination as charismatic, famous and benevolent. These connect up in various ways throughout the chart.

For example, Uranus is in the rulership of that strong Jupiter in the same sign, is conjunct Mercury, and is also in the triplicity and face of Mars. There is a combined influence of all three of those planets here.

Similarly, looking at the Ascendant, it is ruled by Mercury which aspects the Ascendant by sextile. It has dignity for Jupiter in triplicity, term and face. Jupiter is tightly square the Ascendant, and the Ascendant is conjunct Mars. Again the three key planets are linked together.

Family Life

Looking at his family and early life, the fourth house is ruled by Mercury, which we noted is in detriment and fall. Belafonte was born into a poor immigrant family. His parents separated and he was sent to Jamaica as a boy to live with relatives. It was in Jamaica that he experienced firsthand the oppression of blacks by English landowners. Belafonte returned to New York City at age twelve to live with his mother. They struggled in poverty, and Belafonte often stayed with relatives while his mother worked at a variety of low paying jobs. This difficult family background and childhood reflects the fourth house ruler being debilitated.

Venus

The planet Venus is in Aries early in the eleventh house. Venus is in detriment and peregrine.

Venus has strong mutual reception Sun by exaltation and triplicity, and the Sun also has Venus as term ruler. The Sun and Venus are averse, which does not negate their mutual reception, but does make it less conscious and controllable.

Venus is ruled by Mars and is related to his art and how it fits in his chosen community. Venus, the planet of art and song, is in the eleventh house of community, singing sixth house songs of normal folk, and the songs of slaves and the oppressed.

Moon

The Moon in this chart is in Aquarius in the ninth house, about 5 degrees from the Midheaven. By dignity the Moon is largely dominated by Saturn, with Venus having dignity by term and face. The Moon rules the second house.

I think that the Moon here in the ninth house could represent Harry's mother, who sent him far away to live in Jamaica while she stayed and worked in New York, connecting the ninth house of distant travel with the second house of sustenance. Being very near the Midheaven, I think this also represents how Harry admired and idealized his mother, and all of the values of caring that she stood for.

Saturn

Saturn is strong and angular on the cusp of the seventh house of open enemies. Saturn has dignity by triplicity, and is strongly influenced in dignity by Jupiter as ruler and triplicity lord. Saturn also rules the tenth house and the Midheaven which represents the establishment, the ruling class.

Saturn is in a strong applying opposition with peregrine Mars on the Ascendant, less than 4 degree orb.

I think this strong Mars/Saturn opposition sitting right on the Ascendant/Descendant axis is Belafonte's basic stance as peregrine outsider and activist standing up against an oppressive system in power. Belafonte defined himself with his community of blacks against the white establishment.

T Square

The Mars/Saturn opposition is the backbone of the chart. Those two planets form a mutable T square with the very strong Jupiter/Sun conjunction at the point of the T. Jupiter has dignity at all three points in this pattern so it clearly dominates.

We have the metaphor of the basic opposition of civil rights activist against the white oppressor establishment, being made visible through the Jupiter/Sun conjunction - this is Belafonte using his fame as an entertainer to make his civil rights work more visible. His art was a vehicle for his activist work.

Full Aspect Pattern

Note the pattern and symmetry here. We have the T Square building on the base of the Mars/Saturn opposition. On that same base we have a lovely a pair of trines to the end points, Moon to Mars and Venus to Saturn, plus sextiles between each of the intermediate points, Mars, Venus, Moon and Saturn. It is a beautiful mix of stress plus flow. Some of those sextiles are a bit wide by degree, but if you think of aspects as being primarily by whole sign, that intertwined set of aspect patterns includes every one of the seven traditional planets. The T square by sign gets five of the seven planets, and the two trines with sextiles get the other two. Nothing is left out.

Jupiter has dignity at every one of the points in these aspect patterns, and it is the symmetrical center of the entire pattern. We keep coming back to Jupiter as dominating the chart.

Moral Compass

The dignified Jupiter cazimi the Sun stands for what Belafonte called his "moral compass". It is a Jupiterean sense of justice in his heart, and of his being true to his values. That is a beautiful illustration of the meaning of Jupiter cazimi.

Pope Francis

Jorge Mario Bergoglio, December 17, 1936, 9 PM, Buenos Aires, Argentina. Rodden Rating AA. Whole Sign Houses.

Jupiter and Saturn

We begin by noting that Jupiter and Saturn are in mutual reception and are co-dispositors. The two rule the chart together.

Jupiter rules the ninth and the sixth houses and Saturn is in the ninth house. The two planets together, especially Jupiter, represent the state of the Roman Catholic church, and Francis' particular role. As pope, Francis is the church.

Jupiter is the church, and Saturn is a religious body that is old, conservative, rule driven and strict.

Francis' conception of the church unites the sixth and ninth houses ruled by Jupiter. It is the church as servant, spokesperson for the slaves, the outcast, the poor.

Jupiter is also the most debilitated planet in the chart, in fall, combust and out of sect, and it has dignity by face only. Face is a position of service with no authority, a servant. Face is also

153

can signify the church as a facade, showing a face but having no real power. Behind the face it is in fall and keeping up appearances.

There are many ways that Jupiter in fall describes the Catholic church today.

The church is in fall in the sense of losing authority. Jupiter connected to peregrine Saturn shows the church as old-fashioned and out of style, conservative, legalistic and severe. It is out of touch with the modern world and is losing credibility with many of its members for its stand on issues like ordination of women, divorce, and same sex relationships.

A planet in fall also connotes disgrace, and we see clergy sex abuse scandals. The church has lost its trust and credibility, so that many people no longer listen to the church or view it as an authority.

The debility of fall also plays in with the connection between ninth and sixth houses through Francis' vision of the church as servant. Francis identifies with sixth house people, slaves and servants, the powerless, the outcast. Francis gives voice to people in fall. Jupiter with face is a servant claiming no power for itself and identifying with the powerless.

> "I prefer a Church which is bruised, hurting, and dirty because it has been out on the streets, rather than a Church which is unhealthy from being confined and from clinging to its own security."

Face has a double edged meaning. It is the face of a servant, and a face as a facade, appearance only.

Jupiter is antiscia the Sun, closely connecting the two planets, which further strengthens its importance. The Sun in traditional astrology connotes rulership, eminence and authority, so Jupiter antiscia the Sun shows Francis as pope, the titular head or Sun of the Church. The Sun is conjunct the North Node which further magnifies its importance. The Sun in the sixth house is the church and the pope as servant. There is also an aptness to the Sun/Jupiter connection being by antiscia, which is a kind of shadow conjunction - the identity of Francis is swallowed up in the shadow of the church.

Jupiter and Saturn are both in the terms of Mercury so Mercury implements their agenda. Francis was a theologian and seminary teacher before he became Cardinal and then Pope. His writing and speaking and teaching is all in the service of Jupiter and Saturn.

Venus

Venus is the strongest planet in overall dignity together with Mercury, and has dignity by term and face. Venus also has strong mixed mutual reception with Saturn by rulership to exaltation. She dominates both the Midheaven (by ruler, triplicity and term) and Ascendant (by triplicity, term and face).

Venus is how Francis appears to the world.

Venus is strong in this chart, but this is a Venus ruled by Saturn. The man is a peacemaker and compassionate, but this is a stark, severe compassion. Francis is ruled by his beliefs and the laws, and the obedience they impose on him.

Saturn and Venus in mutual reception intertwine in his values. With the strong Saturn Venus mutual reception, rulership to exaltation, there is a solid conservative theology, combined with his dedication to the Venusian ideal of compassion, peace, reconciliation and dialog.

Venus ruled by Saturn fits his lifestyle, severe with no frills, paring down much of the indulgent richness of ornament of the papal role. This includes his his living quarters and his papal dress.

The Moon and Venus together dominate the Ascendant by dignity, and both are averse the Ascendant in the eighth house and ruled by Saturn. Francis is a self-effacing servant. We do not see the personal needs and emotions of this man, we see his principles in action.

 The two Lords of the angles, the Moon at the Ascendant and Venus at the Midheaven, are both ruled by Saturn in the ninth house. We keep coming back to Saturn and Jupiter.

The dignities establish the overall shape of the chart, and the different points we have examined all reinforce each other.

Habemus Papam! Jorge Bergoglio Becomes Pope Francis

This is the chart of the date and time that Francis was elected Pope. It is drawn for the exact time that white smoke arose from the Sistine Chapel, announcing the new pope had been selected.

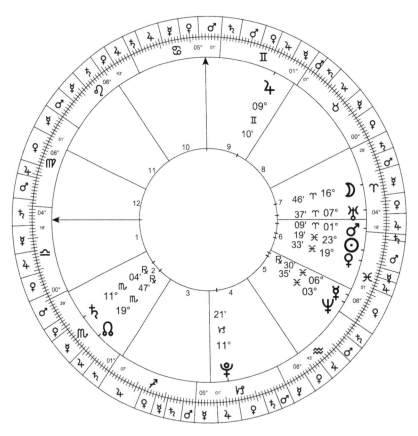

Habemus Papam! March 13, 2013, 7:06 pm, in Vatican City, Rome, Italy. Rating AA

The Midheaven is in Cancer, within 5 degrees of Francis' Ascendant, signifying Francis being raised to prominence and rulership. The Ascendant is Libra, ruled by Venus with Saturn exalted there. The same two planets rule the angles as in his nativity.

Venus represents the person, Jorge Bergoglio, and Venus is combust. This is the man Bergoglio totally burning up his personal identity in his public role as Pope, represented by the Sun. As pope he no longer exists as a private person, he is completely swallowed up by his role.

Mercury is emerging from under the rays retrograde and is now rising before the Sun. Mercury before the Sun is more in the public eye, Francis acting as spokesperson for the church.

The Sun, Venus and Mercury are all in the sixth house, so we see the same sixth house emphasis as in his natal chart.

Mercury in the sixth house and Jupiter in the ninth house are in mutual reception, connecting those houses as in the natal.

Jupiter is at home in the ninth house of the church. Jupiter is in detriment and dominated by Mercury while still having dignity by triplicity, term and face. I think this suggests the church Francis leads is off balance and in detriment, while the 3 minor dignities speak of Francis as an effective and competent leader. The church will likely come together more as a team (triplicity, group, family), get things done a bit better (term), and in addition, Francis puts a friendlier, more jovial, more Jupiterean sort of face on the church. Francis makes the Catholic church appear more welcoming.

Mars is in his rulership in Aries and is angular in the seventh house. Mars also rules the second house where we find Saturn peregrine and retrograde. We can connect this to the troubled financial state of the church at the time Francis took power. I think we can consider Mars in the seventh house ruling the second as Francis threatening some segments of the old church that are trying to hold on to their money, prestige and power.

With Saturn in the second house in bad shape the church could be having financial problems now. The ruler of the second in the seventh points to lawsuits related to clerical sex abuse scandals. Saturn in the second house, rules the fourth and fifth houses. The fourth house could be the church property which is a source of income that also threatened by the lawsuits, and with Saturn in bad shape that property may be getting old and need work. Saturn ruling the fifth house of children and sexual pleasure uncomfortably connotes older (Saturn) men abusing children sexually.

Note how the chart of the selecting of Pope Francis repeats the main themes of the natal chart of Jorge Bergoglio as he assumes the office of Pope. The chart is simultaneously a chart of the man, and of the church as a whole.

William Lilly's House Purchase

This is a very famous horary question from William Lilly's masterpiece, *Christian Astrology*. This is a question Lilly asked for himself about the purchase of a house that he really wanted. I will use this example to illustrate how dignity and debility make sense of this chart. Most of this overlaps with Lilly's analysis, and I am adding a few details of my own concerning the minor dignities. In particular, near the end of this analysis, we will see how the minor dignities, especially terms, add further detail.

I am using the terms of Ptolemy here since that is what Lilly used. Quotes from Lilly are in italic.

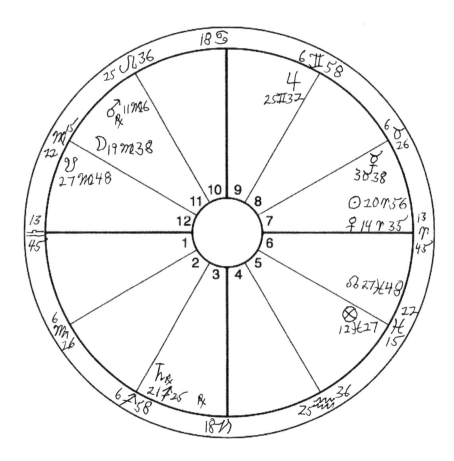

The Inheritance of the house wherein at this present 1647, I live, and some others being proffered me to buy 1634, I had a desire to know if I should deal with the Seller and procure Moneys in convenient time to pay for the Purchase, (my own Money being in such hands as I could not call it in under six months warning) **being desirous, I say, to purchase the said houses, and fully resolved upon it**, *I took my own Question myself, at what time I found my mind was most perplexed and solicitous about it; the time of my Query to myself fell out according to the position of Heaven aforesaid.*

Lilly is represented by the Libra Ascendant and its ruler, Venus. The Descendant represents the seller. The house itself is represented by the fourth house, Capricorn, ruled by Saturn with

Mars exalted.

Venus is in detriment in Aries in the seventh house of the seller. The Sun is the exalted lord of the seventh house and is right there in the seventh. The seller rules this deal and Lilly knows it, so he is expecting to pay a very high price for the house. Mars is the ruler of the seventh house and also rules the second house of money. The seller rules Lilly's money in this transaction.

The house itself is represented by Capricorn and its ruler, Saturn. Lilly is the Libra Ascendant and Saturn is exalted in Libra. Lilly exalts or highly values the house, and has already resolved to purchase it.

(Strictly speaking, by the traditional definition of reception it is Saturn that receives the Libra Ascendant representing Lilly. You could say that the house treats Lilly as an honored and valued person - in other words, the house will be good to Lilly.)

Saturn, the house itself, is in mixed condition, being retrograde and in a weak cadent house. The building was very old and did have some problems. Saturn is averse the fourth house so there may be some issues of neglect by the owner.

Looking at the minor dignities, Saturn has dignity by term and by face. (If you use all three triplicity rulers, Saturn also has dignity by triplicity here.) Two minor dignities is the equivalent of one major dignity. The house is in basically good shape (equivalent of major dignity), is still very functional (terms) and has a good appearance or facade (face).

The quality of the houses are signified by Capricorn the sign of the 4th, and Saturn Lord of the 4th, who having no material debilities, except Retrogradation and Cadency, also being in Trine with Sun; the houses were really old, but strong and able to stand many years.

The Sun or owner is trine the house, and Venus or Lilly is applying to a trine aspect. The house passes from Sun to Venus, and this trine was one of the main indicators Lilly used to confirm that he would succeed in buying the house.

When Venus and Sun came to Conjunction in Taurus, that day I bargained, viz. die Venus 25 April following: the 17 of May Venus and Moon in Conjunction; I paid 530 £, and my conveyance was Sealed.

The transfer of ownership is represented by the conjunction of Sun and Venus, seller and buyer. The transaction was completed when Venus had moved into Taurus, where Venus had rulership. That is when Lilly became lord of the house.

If you look at the dignity of term, we find something very interesting here: **The Sun, Mercury, Venus and Mars are all in the terms of Venus, who represents Lilly**. The major parties in the deal are in Lilly's terms. Lilly is doing everything he can to engineer this sale so that it goes through. **He doesn't control the price of the house, but he is in charge of the execution (terms) of the deal.** Term is all about getting things done.

There is another detail of minor dignity that I want to note here. Lilly's second house of finances is Scorpio, ruled by Mars in the eleventh house of friends, and Mars is retrograde. Lilly's own money was tied up, and he knew he would not be able to get to it in time to buy the house. ***However, note that Mars is in Virgo where Venus and Mars both have dignity by triplicity. Venus and Mars are in the same tribe, and Lilly was able to borrow the needed money from a friend.*** Triplicity is good fortune or support from family or tribe.

There is another possible meaning of triplicity here. As we noted, Mars is the ruler of the seventh house, the seller. ***and Lilly notes that he was good friends with the daughter of the seller, who helped him put the transaction through.*** This is triplicity as good fortune and support through friends and family.

Was it a good purchase? I will let William Lilly have the last word here.

The truth of the matter is, I had a hard bargain, as the Figure every way considered doth manifest, and shall never live to see many of the leases yet in being, expired: and as Venus is in Aries, viz. opposite to her own House, so did I do myself injury by the Bargain, I mean in matter of Money. But the love I bore to the House I now live in, wherein I lived happily with a good master full seven years, therein obtained my first Wife, and was bountifully blessed by God with the Goods of this World therein, made me neglect a small hindrance, nor now, I thank God, do I repent it; finding Gods blessing in a plentiful measure upon my Labors.

Dignity Gone Bad - Jeffrey Dahmer

If you are going to work with the system of dignities, you need to be able to make sense of Jeffrey Dahmer's chart.

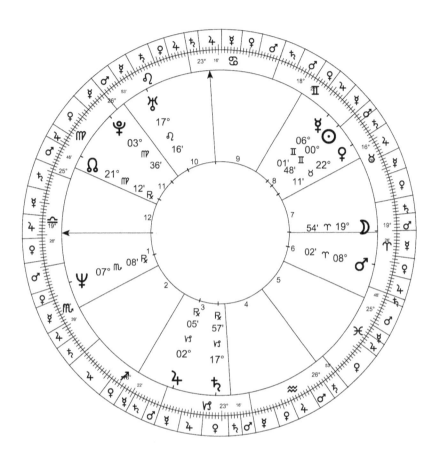

Jeffrey Lionel Dahmer, May 21, 1960, Milwaukee, Wisconsin. Rodden Rating AA. Placidus houses.

At first glance if you look at just the essential dignities, it looks like this should be a really strong chart. ***There are four planets in their rulership.*** Going in order around the houses there is Saturn in Capricorn, Mars in Aries, Venus in Libra and Mercury in Gemini. Having that many planets in rulership is quite unusual, and is a propitious sign.

So what went wrong?

This chart is a case where you have to use the full system of dignities, essential and accidental, to really make sense of the chart. The first time I ran this chart through the full *Cheate Sheete* checklist I was surprised to find that most of the planets ended up with very low scores, and most of the low scoring was caused by accidental dignity factors. (I encourage you to do your own analysis of the chart to see if you concur.)

The only two reasonably positive planets are Saturn and then Mars, the two malefics. The weakest planets, with negative scores, are the two lights, the Sun and the Moon - and, Venus.

Accidental dignity affects more than just form. It also has a strong effect on quality, especially when debilities are cumulative. That is what we find here.

Elements and Modes

Looking at elemental balance Dahmer's chart has three planets in air, two fire, two water, and nothing in earth. Looking at the modes the chart has four cardinal, three mutable, and no fixed. The angles are both cardinal so the chart has a complete lack of fixity or stability. You will also see a theme of lack of support as we go through the chart.

House Placement

Looking at just the traditional planets, only the Moon is in a strong angular house.

Four of the seven planets are in negative houses. Venus, Sun and Mercury are in the eighth and Mars is in the sixth. Two of the remaining three traditional planets, Saturn and Jupiter, are weak and cadent in the third house.

Six of the seven traditional planets are in negative or weak houses. The overall pattern is very weak.

So what of the one angular planet? It is one of the two weakest planets in the chart - the Moon.

The Moon

The only planet in an angular house is the Moon, right on the cusp of the seventh house. The Moon is the only planet that faces outward to the world, which makes it particularly exposed and vulnerable. And, as we shall see, the Moon is one of two planets that are in particularly bad shape.

The Moon here is peregrine, out of sect, and waning. It is in Aries, a cold wet planet in a hot dry sign. It is a complete elemental mismatch.

What is particularly negative here is that the Moon is in a tight separating square with retrograde Saturn in Capricorn in the third house.

Looking at the reception in that square, the Moon is in the sign of Saturn's fall, and Saturn is in the sign of the Moon's detriment. It is doubly negative. There is mutual reception by triplicity between them, but this does not override the mutual hostile lack of reception between them. The reception is hostile, and this aggravates the negative effects of the square. The reception by triplicity likely means this plays out through members of his family and tribe.

Saturn is in the tenth house from the Moon, an overcoming square. With Saturn being the stronger of the two planets the Moon is devastated by Saturn.

Dahmer is reported to have been sexually abused by an uncle or neighbor when he was a child. Saturn here is in the third house of related family and neighbors, and we noted the mutual reception by triplicity.

The only other close aspect the Moon makes is a separating trine from Uranus in Leo in the tenth house. I would not look to that for emotional support.

The Moon at 19 Aries in this chart is void of course. It gets no help from any other aspects for the rest of its course in Aries. Again we see lack of support.

Being the only angular planet, the vulnerable Moon that faces the world is wounded and unsupported.

The other major weak point is the key to the entire chart – the planet Venus.

Venus

On the plus side Venus has dignity by rulership and triplicity, and it is direct. On the minus side Venus is out of sect in the eighth house, oriental and moving towards the Sun.

Venus is moving towards combustion.

How negative or positive combustion is depends on the dignity of the planet and the dignity of the Sun, and of their reception of each other. In this chart the Sun is peregrine. Venus is in her rulership at 22 Taurus, but *she reaches her conjunction with the Sun at very early Gemini, where she has no dignity at all*. She goes from rulership and triplicity to peregrine and burnt in the space of a degree. It is abrupt, like falling off a cliff.

If we are correct, that there is a connection between Venus going combust and whatever went wrong with Dahmer, then we should see some kind of defining event mirrored in astrology timing techniques. I looked at the primary directions for the time when Venus reached conjunction with the Sun. At the age the direction was exact, Dahmer had a double hernia injury to his scrotum that required a serious operation, and that caused him a lot of severe pain both before and after the operation. According to his father he was never the same after that event. He became tense, withdrawn, isolated and lacking in self-confidence.

The Ascendant of this chart is Libra. Venus is the ruler of the Ascendant, so in traditional terms *Venus is Jeffrey Dahmer.*

Fixed Stars

There are two nasty fixed stars that affect this point in the chart, one in a tight aspect, and the other close enough to pay attention to.

One of them, Alcyone in the Pleiades, is at very late Taurus or early Gemini where Venus joins the Sun in combustion. Pleiades is the constellation of the weeping sisters, causing injury and sorrow. Some texts describe Alcyone as giving you something to cry about. In this case that is literal - Dahmer spent a lot of time crying in serious pain from his injury.

The other fixed star to note here is Algol, which is around 26 Taurus. That is a four degree orb from either Venus or the Moon. It is also at the midpoint of the Sun and Venus. Midpoints are not used much in traditional astrology, but I have found them to be powerful and significant. The symbolism of Algol includes beheading and bodies being chopped up. I would not hang the entire chart interpretation on this one fixed star, but if you accept either the midpoint or the wide orb, it is a frightening supporting factor.

Venus Combust

Combustion in this case correlates to the major injury that caused Dahmer to become very withdrawn. Combustion also connotes being hidden, taken out of public view, and this is in the hidden eighth house. That fits his becoming withdrawn, and it also fits activities hidden from public view. This combustion takes place in the eighth house which is associated with death, including dead bodies.

Venus is also the planet related to sexual pleasure. Debilitated Venus, eighth house, combust - hidden sexual activities involving dead bodies.

Other Patterns

We have covered the critical points in Dahmer's chart at this point, but there are a couple of other points that are worth noting.

Looking again at that vulnerable Moon it is in the seventh house. That Moon does not just relate to Dahmer. Being in the seventh house it also represents his victims.

We mentioned that Venus is lord of the Ascendant, but it is worth noting that the almuten of the Ascendant is Saturn, who has dignity there by exaltation, triplicity and face. You could also take Saturn to represent Dahmer. In that case Saturn square Moon describes his encounters with his partners and victims.

Essential dignities are very important, but they need to be used in combination in the entire context of essential and accidental dignities. Accidental dignity is not just about strength and prominence, it also can affect quality.

Hermann Hesse

I was in high school and college when Hermann Hesse was at his most popular during the late 1960's and early 1970's, and his main novels were pretty much required reading if you considered yourself hip, aware and with it. The name of his novel *Steppenwolf* entered popular culture through the rock band by the same name, with their signature anthem, *Born to Be Wild* (which coined the phrase, Heavy Metal) - an association that would have thoroughly dismayed Hesse. He did feel that the book *Steppenwolf* was the most misunderstood of his works - he was not glorifying the shadow in that book, he was trying to face and learn of it in order to transcend it.

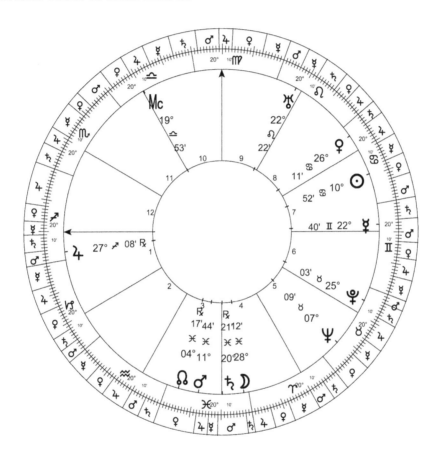

Hermann Hesse, July 2, 1877, 6:30 PM, Calw, Germany. Rodden Rating AA. Placidus Houses.

Books like *Demian* and *Steppenwolf* spoke to the rebelliousness of the sixties, and books like *Journey to the East* and *Siddhartha* spoke to our hunger for exotic spiritual paths from the East. Looking back, I suspect we understood very little of what Hesse was actually saying - and I don't think we would have particularly liked it had we really understood it.

Hesse's family, his life, his writing, his philosophy, and his physical illnesses are all of a piece, all different expressions of the same pattern of inward division and rebellious turmoil, with an attempt to reach healing and transcendence through detached mental contemplation.

General

First, note the chart has no fixity at all. There are no fixed signs for planets or for the major angles, nor are there any planets or angles in earth.

Hesse has five planets in water, one fire and one air planet, and none in earth. In addition, five of the seven traditional planets are mutable, two are cardinal, and none are fixed. The Ascendant is mutable and the Midheaven is cardinal, so there are no fixed angles. This chart is extremely mutable, introspective and unearthly, with an abstract mystical vagueness.

The majority of the planets are below the horizon, and there are no planets that are within sixty degrees of the Midheaven on either side. When we look at aspect patterns later, you will see that the entire aspect pattern of the chart points downward. This reinforces the introspective, secluded, abstract, and mental qualities of the chart.

Jupiter

Looking at the angles, in the first house we have Jupiter in Sagittarius in his rulership rising, and in the seventh house we have Mercury in his rulership in Gemini right on the house cusp. These are the only two planets in their rulership, and they form an opposition. This axis is the backbone of the entire chart. The two planets Jupiter and Mercury, having associations with thought, philosophy, religion and spiritual values, dominate this very mutable, un-earthly, un-physical chart.

Looking at reception, Jupiter receives Mercury in triplicity only, but there is no reception from Mercury to Jupiter. Each planet is in the other's detriment, so this is an especially difficult opposition.

If you look at the chain of dispositors in this chart, all of the planets report to Jupiter as final dispositor except for Mercury.

With the Placidus house system Jupiter rules the twelfth and third houses along with the first, and Mercury rules the sixth and ninth houses along with seventh. The connection with the reclusive and cadent sixth and twelfth houses seems appropriate, as is the connection with the third to ninth house axis of communication, writing, teaching, religion and philosophy.

When you have the same ruler for the first and twelfth houses, as with Jupiter here, the two houses become intertwined, and the sense of self takes on a twelfth house dimension, pointing to Hesse's reclusive, ascetic, world-denying side. Jupiter is also the natural significator of religion, law, and philosophy. Hesse's entire life was defined by his strict religious upbringing.

Mercury

The opposing planet Mercury is in the seventh house, and rules the neighboring sixth house as well as the ninth. There is a connection of Mercury with philosophy and religion. This also suggests that Hesse's primary relationships will have a mental and philosophical dimension.

Along with the opposition to the very dominant Jupiter in the 1st house, Mercury has other problems here. Mercury is making a heliacal setting, being 18 degrees away from the Sun while moving towards him and going under the rays. It is significant that Mercury will change signs into Cancer before reaching the Sun, which means he loses all dignity before the combustion, and that can be very negative. A planet's dignity can make a lot of difference as to how debilitating combustion is, and in this chart Mercury is peregrine and homeless as it plunges into the Sun's furnace. Mercury is being burned up.

Since Mercury is in the seventh house, this is clearly related to his wife who was increasingly mentally ill and had episodes of psychosis - going under the rays and towards combustion is an apt metaphor for your mind being burned up. Hesse himself also had periods of mental illness for which he was institutionalized. We will see more on the connection between Mercury and physical and mental illness later, when we consider the planet in the context of the aspects it makes.

Mercury in the seventh house is in a mutable sign, which can indicate multiple marriages, and Hesse was married three times. It appears all marriages had primarily a mental and intellectual kind of bond, and all three appear to have had an unstable and mutable quality.

Saturn

Saturn, the out of sect malefic, is debilitated in this chart. It is retrograde and peregrine, in the weak and cadent third house.

Saturn is in a loose trine aspect with the Sun, and outer planets in trine to the Sun are often near one of their stations. In this case, if you look in the ephemeris, you will see that Saturn is very nearly exactly at first station. The ephemeris marks Saturn as turning retrograde the day before Hesse's birth. Planets in station are greatly emphasized in intensity and importance, and first station is very much the more negative of the two stations since the planet is just starting to go retrograde.

Saturn at first station is an intense repressive force, and it is often turned inwards, especially in a cadent house. Hesse had a severe and ascetic religious upbringing from Pietist missionary parents, who expected their son to continue their work and go into the ministry.

Saturn is down at the bottom of the chart, in the third house with Placidus houses, and in the fourth house by whole sign. In terms of aspects, *Saturn is in a square with Mercury, with the Ascendant, and with Jupiter in the first house*.

Saturn rules the second house from within the third house, which points to income from writing and intellectual pursuits. Much of Capricorn is in the first house, so this will put a Saturnine cast to Hesse's self-image.

Both the Ascendant and Midheaven are in the face of Saturn, as is Jupiter rising, and Saturn displays much of the face that Hesse turned towards the world - cold, reclusive, detached and serious.

The Moon

The Moon is in Pisces, with dignity by triplicity. The most important fact about the Moon is that it is conjunct Saturn, and loosely conjunct Mars in the same sign. By dignity, the Moon is in the terms of Saturn, and the triplicity and face of Mars, and Mars and Saturn are in the triplicity of the Moon. With the shared dignity by triplicity and this group being down at the bottom of the chart, I think this points to a stressed family environment, with the severe influence of Saturn and Mars predominating.

Looking at Mercury and Moon in square, Moon is in the detriment and fall of Mercury, and Mercury is not received by the Moon at all. This is a very negative and stressful square - it is likely that Hesse's intellect viewed emotions as a form of weakness that were to be criticized, analyzed and then detached from. This detachment expressed as an impersonal coldness. His intellect and emotions were working at cross purposes.

Mars

The planet Mars is also in Pisces along with Saturn and the Moon, with dignity by triplicity. He is on the cusp of the third house, and rules the fourth and eleventh houses. In the latter part of his life Hesse had a home provided to him by neighbors - third house people offered him a fourth house home.

As with the Moon, the most important feature of Mars in this chart is its conjunction with Saturn and the Moon. The Mars to Saturn conjunction is mutually applying, each moving towards the other with Saturn retrograde. Mutual application is generally considered to be a very negative condition, and we will see multiple ways that it plays out in Hesse's life.

This conjunction displayed as a strong rebellious streak against any sort of religious or spiritual authority. Later in his life it was evident in his rebellion against the militant nationalism that swept Germany in the Nazi era of the 1930's.

We have looked at Saturn, Mars and the Moon separately, and now we need to consider them together. Mars, Saturn and the Moon are loosely conjunct in the same sign, with Saturn peregrine and Mars and the Moon with dignity by triplicity only. Neither Mars nor the Moon have any reception to Saturn.

Saturn is conjunct Mars and is in the triplicity, term and face of Mars, but Saturn receives Mars only by face. Saturn conjunct Moon can mean depression and deeply repressed emotion, and Mars and Saturn conjunct can mean repressed anger and aggression, and also repressed physical, vital and sexual energy. This is shown in Hesse's strict and puritanical church upbringing. It is reflected in his spirituality which is sex negative, world-denying, and denying of feelings, all of which were cosidered to be inferior, and to be detached from and transcended.

Mars and Moon together, especially Mars, were probably what he would have considered his shadow. Mars is the dark aggressive, animal and sexual side, and the Moon is the vulnerable feminine side. Neither has any real acceptance in Hesse's conscious attitude or in his mature philosophy.

Hesse had ongoing problems with depression, and with nervous problems, eye problems and severe headaches. We see the stress on his Moon and on his Mercury in this configuration. Mercury rules the sixth house of illness. Mercury going under the Sun is likely related to his ongoing eye problems. Mercury and Gemini in the sixth house are related to nervous diseases.

That Horrid T Square

We have now have all the pieces in place to look at the full T-square configuration. We have Mercury and Jupiter in opposition with no reception, and at the point we have Mars, Saturn and Moon conjunct; the Saturn restriction on his sensitive Moon feelings and his Mars animal self. It is the clash of those three forces that is fought out in the battleground of Hesse's life, in his physical symptoms, and in his writing.

Probably the most distinctive and popular of Hesse's works in the 1960's was *Steppenwolf*, where he is wrestling with that dark Mars energy. Hesse developed a strategy to transcend that animal side through an attitude of detachment and gentle humor, symbolized in *Steppenwolf* by the classical music of Mozart.

In this configuration Jupiter is only planet that has dignity at all of the points in the T square.

Jupiter and Saturn have a strong mixed mutual reception with Jupiter dominating. I think we can see a strong Saturnian influence here that gave Hesse a strict ascetic and Stoic worldview, having affinity with Schopenhauer, and with Buddhist philosophy teaching the superiority of renouncing the world. The Moon has no dignity with either Jupiter or Mercury. We have abstract intellect here, completely at odds with, and distancing from, his emotions.

Mercury also comes out poorly in dignity in this configuration. He has no dignity with any of the other planets. Jupiter is in Mercury's detriment, and the other 3 planets are in Pisces, his detriment and fall. Even with his being in his rulership, Mercury is weak, isolated and embattled in this chart. We see the effect in Hesse's mental problems, his wife's psychosis, and his ongoing problems with headaches and depression.

Venus

Hesse's Venus is in Cancer, with dignity by triplicity only, right on the cusp of the eighth house. Venus is the ruler of Hesse's Midheaven, so she rules his presence in the world, his career and reputation, and Hesse was a fiction writer. Venus also rules his fifth house, and since Hesse did not have any children, his fifth house expressed as his creativity in his fictional works.

We have already looked at Hesse's T square that has five of the planets in his chart. The center point of the configuration, the Saturn, Mars and Moon conjunction, is all trine to Venus in the eighth house. I think the highly stressed point of the T works out much of its energy through this trine to Venus, through his art and creativity. Venus is on cusp of the eighth house by Placidus, and also rules the tenth house of his vocation and his fame as a creative writer.

Hesse's art expresses the struggle of a revolt against deadness and oppression, combined with a horror for the baser, more vulnerable and more violent aspects of human experience. Hesse seeks release and healing through an abstract and detached spiritual transcendence which became more marked in his later work.

The Angles

Circling back to look at dignity at the angles, the Ascendant is ruled by Jupiter, and the Descendant by Mercury. The Midheaven is ruled by Venus, but Saturn and Jupiter are strong by dignity at both the Ascendant and Midheaven. *Jupiter is the one planet with dignity at all four of the angles*, another sign of the dominance of this planet.

This chart is a very vivid picture of how Hesse's philosophy, his physical condition, his marriages, and his health challenges are all of a piece, all intertwined. He used the intense internal struggle to create powerful philosophical fiction.

Arthur Schopenhauer

Doing this chart analysis of the German philosopher Schopenhauer was a lot of fun for me, partly because Schopenhauer is one of my favorite philosophers to read for pleasure. His thinking has a lot of affinity with Stoicism, which I like, and he also happens to be a very beautiful writer and clear thinker. Analyzing the chart made me smile, because I can see the man's writing and philosophy, and also what an interesting and unpleasant character he was as a person. The chart is almost comically extreme, larger than life, and yet all-too-human in its mix of strengths and weaknesses. You could say that I love and admire him the more for that mix.

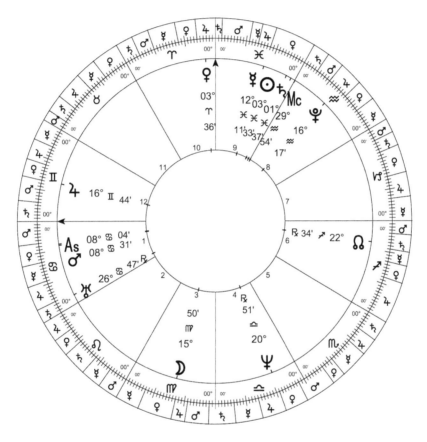

Arthur Schopenhauer, February 22, 1788, 12 PM, Danzig, Germany. Rodden Rating AA.

General

Looking at essential dignity, there are no planets in rulership or exaltation, 3 in detriment (Venus, Jupiter and Mercury), and 2 in fall (Mercury and Mars). ***That is 4 out of the 7 traditional planets with a major essential debility.*** This means that debility sets the tone for the entire chart. Recall that debility has to do with being out of balance, not feeling at home here, and fall in particular relates to feeling ignored, disrespected, not listened to. This exactly describes the general tone of his attitude and experience for most of his life, living alone and in obscurity in a little apartment paid for by a small inheritance.

Detriment and fall can indicate an outsider mentality - he felt both ignored and despised, and he returned the favor by despising the German culture around him. His philosophy was very much at odds with the prevailing schools in Germany in his lifetime, and he deliberately and abrasively took an outside stance.

Looking at the balance of elements we have four planets in water, and one in each of the other elements. Looking at the modes there are five planets in mutable signs, with two cardinal and no fixed. The lack of fixity is further emphasized by house placement; note that five of the seven planets are in cadent houses by whole sign. This emphasis on mutability in cadent houses is appropriate for a philosopher. It also fits the tone of his philosophy, which states that all of our experience is necessarily a product of thought. There is no physical fixity in Schopenhauer's world.

The only fixity in the entire chart is the Midheaven, which is very late in Aquarius. Assuming the birth time is correct, it is only 5 minutes or one-twelfth of a degree away from Pisces. If he was born at the recorded hour of 12 pm or slightly before, the Midheaven would be Aquarius. Had he been born even one minute later, the Midheaven would be in Pisces. There is instability even in this one point of stability.

Saturn is tightly conjunct the Midheaven in very early Pisces. The combined effect of fixed Midheaven plus Saturn was strong enough to make his life routine very stable and unchanging - his philosophy was essentially unchanged throughout his life, and his daily routine was a rigid as clockwork, with a fixed time daily for dining, writing, playing flute, and taking the same length walk at the same time every day regardless of the weather. It is an interesting mix of a stable life routine and structure, with a philosophy that emphasized change and impermanence.

Mars

Note that we have the two malefic planets each tightly conjunct an angle.

On the Ascendant we have Mars in Cancer, in his fall. This is a person who feels ignored and slighted, is rude and ill-tempered, and acts in unbalanced ways both to get attention and to scare it away. It is tightly conjunct the Ascendant, so Mars is very prominent, in your face. Mars in fall here on the Ascendant describes an arrogant, irritable and critical personality. Mars in fall is also his conviction that no-one listened to him or took him seriously, and that was true for most of his life.

Mars is related by Antiscia to the South Node in the 12th house with approximately a one degree orb. This is the first of multiple markers in the chart for his philosophy of world denial and self-negation. The 12th house has that self-negating quality, and the South Node is a malefic point that sucks the life out of things - at the South Node energy is moving away from manifestation and inward, more towards thought and abstraction.

Mars in fall rules the tenth house of reputation, and reflects his total obscurity until very late in his life. This also shows as his arrogance in presenting himself as the most brilliant philosopher in Germany, but at complete odds with the prevailing schools of philosophy. Schopenhauer briefly had a post as teacher and lecturer in a university. The philosopher Hegel was at the peak of his popularity at that time, and Schopenhauer made a point of scheduling his lectures at the same time as Hegel's, and he presented only his own philosophy. The lectures were poorly attended and he lost his teaching post.

Debilitated Mars also rules the fifth house. Schopenhauer never had any children that lived, but he was known for being a Don Juan character who had a constant series of sexual liaisons, and likely he got little in emotional closeness or support from these affairs. Further, in Dresden in 1819, Schopenhauer fathered an illegitimate daughter with a servant. The child died the same year.

We will pick up on where Mars fits in aspect patterns later in the discussion, after we have examined some of the other planets.

Saturn

Saturn, the other malefic, has dignity by face only, and is conjunct the Midheaven within around two degrees. Saturn is in very early Pisces, and rules the Midheaven which is in very late Aquarius. Saturn is both conjunct and averse the Midheaven, strong, important and angular, and yet with the aversion quality of lacking control.

The two malefics, either debilitated or with weak dignity, are closely conjunct the two angles.

Saturn is further weakened here by being combust, conjunct the Sun within around two degrees. Saturn with dignity only by face conjunct the Sun makes for a gloomy, grouchy, bad-tempered recluse.

Saturn in face here can also be taken fairly literally. Saturn is the appearance, the face that he showed the world. It shows in the seriousness and the pessimism of his philosophy, and it showed in his personality.

Saturn rules the seventh house, which delays or denies marriage. It seems he was unable to get really close to people or to form close friendships. Saturn was the face he put on in one to one relationships.

Sun Saturn conjunct on the Midheaven, Mars in fall on the Ascendant - meet Arthur Schopenhauer!

Jupiter and Mercury

This next configuration is the organizing principle of the entirety of Schopenhauer's philosophy, his work and his life.

Jupiter and Mercury are in mutual reception, Gemini to Pisces, each from their debility, and they are also final co-dispositors. My experience is that planets in mutual reception that are co-dispositors like this will dominate the chart, since all the other planets report back to these two.

Having Mercury and Jupiter in mutual reception is common among writers and philosophers, other examples being the 20th century astrologer, philosopher and composer Dane Rudhyar, and the writer Jane Austen.

Mercury is in the ninth house in mutual reception with Jupiter in the twelfth house. Linking the meanings of those two houses, the foundation of this man's life and thought is a philosophy of self-negation. This is the heart of the man.

Along with the strong mutual reception, Jupiter and Mercury are in a tight applying square, ninth to twelfth houses. That square catches some of the tension in this man's philosophy and life. On the one hand he loved music, played flute daily for over an hour, and wrote beautiful poetic prose, some of it on the beauty and importance of music. On the other hand he preached a philosophy of total self-negation, a total renunciation of the will, a renunciation which he never cared to practice in his own life.

Mercury has no dignity, and is dominated by Jupiter as ruler, term and face. Jupiter has dignity by triplicity only. Jupiter is also conjunct the South Node, which further emphasizes the self-denying aspects of his philosophy. We also saw this connection with Mars being Antiscia the South Node, so the two reinforce each other.

Mercury is antiscia Neptune within 3 degrees. I think we can see this reflected in the Buddhist, somewhat mystical slant to his philosophy, where all of experience is only a representation or image or idea in your consciousness. This is not a very strong antiscia connection, but I think it adds suggestive detail.

With Jupiter in the twelfth house and Mercury in the ninth, the man was a philosopher and a recluse.

T Square

The major aspect pattern in this chart is a T square, Mercury in the ninth house opposite the Moon in the third house, with both squaring Jupiter in twelfth house. Here we see the head/heart separation (Mercury to Moon) expressed in his strict self-negating philosophy (Jupiter squaring both from the 12th house conjunct the South Node.)

Mercury dominates in the opposition with the Moon, and there is no mutual reception between the Moon and Jupiter. The Moon is in the detriment of Jupiter. I think of this as a reverse of reception. It shows a hostile attitude of Jupiter towards the Moon. Detriment means that Jupiter would work in a way that would break down or hinder the Moon. Add in the fact that the Moon is down at the bottom of the chart in a cadent house, and it is clear that the Moon comes out in the weakest shape of the planets in the T-square.

This weak Moon is the sign ruler of the Ascendant, overshadowed in power by Mars, but the ruler nevertheless. I picture the sensitive but very self-doubting and self-critical man that hid behind his abrasive exterior. Externally, that Moon played out in his hostile relationship with his mother and his poor attitude towards women in general, a theme that we will see repeated elsewhere.

The only close friends he had were his poodles, and he owned a series of them in the course of his life. Note that the dominant Jupiter also rules the sixth house of small animals. They were one of the outlets for expression of the tension on Jupiter.

With Placidus houses, the Moon is in the fourth house of parents. I think the weak Moon in house four represents the mother he hated and criticized so much, but who paid his way through much of his life. Mars in fall in Cancer is a reflection of this attitude.

With Saturn, the Sun and Mercury within 12 degrees of each other, plus Mercury and the Moon, this one aspect pattern includes five of the seven traditional planets. The dominating point in the pattern is Jupiter, his twelfth house philosophy.

Mars, Moon, Mercury

Mars is sextile the Moon and trine Mercury, the two planets in opposition. Mars in this aspect acts as a point of resolution and harmony, where the tension of the opposition is expressed. That tension of the opposition between intellect and emotion, head and heart, was expressed in the abrasive quality of Mars in fall.

Venus

The one other major planet we have not yet examined is Venus, who is in her detriment in Aries in the tenth house. If you look at the major aspect patterns, the opposition with the T square and the trine and sextile aspects to Mars, Venus stands off to the side. In fact, Venus is averse five of the six other traditional planets, having no relation to them. The only aspect Venus makes is a loose applying square to Mars.

I think that Venus here relates to is poor relations with his mother, and with women in general. He had a strong and active sex drive, where he needed women as sex partners but had no emotional closeness to them.

Venus in fall in Aries in the tenth house is the exalted ruler of Pisces in the ninth house. Venus also has dignity by triplicity in Pisces, and triplicity shows family connections and support. Schopenhauer's mother was a popular fiction writer. He was able to get his books published because of his mother's connection with her publishing house, who published his books as a favor to his mother. His mother was exalted by the publishers in the ninth house. The books Schopenhauer published sold poorly during his lifetime, but late in his life and afterwards they became significant sellers for the publisher.

The Sun in Pisces and Venus in Aries are in mutual exaltation, but they are averse. I think this relates to his exaltation of art in his philosophy.

While the Sun and Venus have mutual exaltation, Saturn in Pisces is received by Venus in exaltation, but Saturn returns the favor by receiving Venus in his fall, and thus devaluing Venus. There is a severe saturnine side to his aesthetic sense. Art gave a desire-less, unattached contemplation, which is a very saturnine sort of approach to aesthetics. The two conjunct planets, Sun and Saturn, show a conflicting relationship with Venus which is mirrored in the contradictions in Schopenhauer's attitude towards art, and towards women.

The Bounds

There are some interesting patterns if you look at the dignity of the bounds.

Venus is in the bounds of Jupiter, and Jupiter in the bounds of Venus, giving mutual reception by bound. I think this connects to the emphasis on aesthetics, on art and music in his philosophy. This re-emphasizes the Sun/Venus mutual reception. Mutual reception between the two benefics by bound could also be related to the beauty of his writing.

Overall the bounds are very much dominated by Venus, who has dignity by bound with five of the seven traditional planets plus the Ascendant. This further fits the emphasis on aesthetics, the beauty of his writing, the fact that his philosophy strongly appeals to many artists, and the fact that he played flute and highly valued music as the highest and purest of the arts. He viewed art and music as the highest expression of his philosophy, the dignity of bound having to do with how you express yourself.

In this chart we see the major themes in his life showing up in multiple places. The self-negating philosophy is in the Mercury Jupiter sixth house connection, and again in Saturn on the Midheaven conjunct the Sun. This connects to the debilitated, abrasive Mars at the Ascendant, where he acted in self-fulfilling ways to make sure he was ignored.

It is very easy to see the man's personality mirrored in the chart, his lack of social life or close relationships, the frequent affairs. It is also easy to see the shape of his very severe philosophy of self-negation.

A very great philosopher, writer and thinker, a lonely, sensitive, reclusive and abrasive human being, and an inspiration to many including me - behold the philosopher and the man, Arthur Schopenhauer.

Maya Angelou

Maya Angelou is poet, writer, and civil rights activist, and is best known for the first in her extended series of autobiographies, *I Know Why the Caged Bird Sings*.

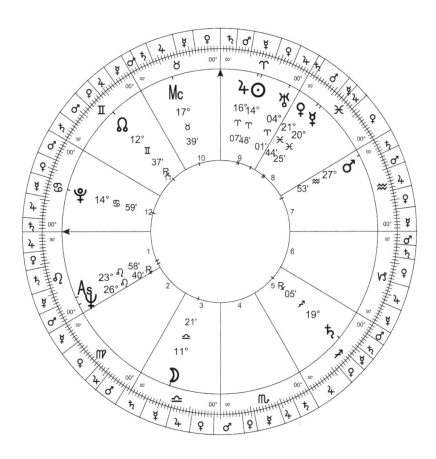

Marguerite Ann Johnson, April 4, 1928, 2:10 PM, St Louis, Missouri. Rodden Rating AA.

The rulers of the Ascendant and Midheaven, Sun and Venus, are both exalted. That is itself a signature for fame. Also, with this very strong Sun exalted, she is as famous as a person as she is for what she wrote or did.

By sign, the Sun is trine the Ascendant, and Venus is sextile the Midheaven. The angular rulers are strong both by dignity and by smooth aspect to the angles.

Sun and Jupiter Together

The center of the chart is the Sun/Jupiter conjunction in the ninth house. It is in Aries, the Sun's exaltation. The ninth house relates to writing, teaching and world travel, and her life abundantly includes all of those. She described herself as a teacher who writes.

Jupiter is combust and is approaching conjunction with the Sun. The negative effects are mitigated by the Sun being dignified by rulership and triplicity, and by Sun and Jupiter having mutual reception by triplicity. Jupiter combust here could also mean that the outer effect of Jupiter was weakened, and its inner effect was intensified. We see the effects of Jupiter through her solar identity.

The Jupiter/Sun conjunction gave her an unshakable optimism and sense of self-worth, and she was a proponent of the positive thinking and mental healing movement. This conjunction resonates with a positive philosophy that gives power to the mind and to words to influence reality.

Venus and Mercury Together

For Angelou's writing and art, we need to consider the Venus/Mercury conjunction in the eighth house, a house which is considered negative and is related to suffering, to fear and to powerlessness.

Mercury is in detriment and fall, while Venus in exaltation and triplicity, so Venus very clearly predominates here. Her Mercury writing comes completely out of the Venus artistic perception. This is not the objectivity of a scientist, it is deeply emotional and artistic.

Mercury rules the second house, and her main income was from her writing.

Mercury is square Saturn, and Mercury receives Saturn in bounds. I think this shows her life strategy of processing her past, and any suffering she experiences, in terms of her writing. The art of writing is the method she uses to cope with and to create her life. Saturn plus Mercury is also good for discipline, form and hard work in writing.

The Sun, Moon, Jupiter, Saturn and Ascendant are all in the bounds of Mercury. This is a remarkably high predominance of one planet in bounds. The dignity of bound has to do with specific implementation, with how things get done. Mercury dominating the bounds is appropriate for a writer writer.

Moon

The Moon is peregrine in Libra, and is dominated by Saturn. The Moon is opposite the strong Sun Jupiter conjunction. She cultivated the kind of mental attitude that admits of no defeat, of no weakness, that is constantly showing strength and optimism. We see the Jupiter optimism opposite the peregrine Moon, so the more she suffered, the more she pushed herself with that fiery Sun and Jupiter optimistic outlook.

With Saturn strongly influencing the Moon there was great pressure to discipline her emotional needs. It is quite optimistic in some ways, and in other ways it is quite severe. Note that Saturn and Moon have mutual reception by face, which I think plays out as her putting on a strong appearance in the face of suffering and vulnerable feelings. It has a stoic feeling to it.

Late in life she stated that we can admit we have defeats, but we must never admit defeat. That is Saturn disciplining her Moon in the service of the Sun/Jupiter optimism.

Moon and Mercury Antiscia - the Shadow Conjunction

The Venus Mercury conjunction is her artistic creation, which uses the events of her life as their subject. Mercury and the Moon are averse, they don't directly connect by any aspect. However, they are conjunct by antiscia within a two degree orb. Antiscia is a shadow connection, like looking at someone in a mirror.

This antiscia, shadow sort of connection between Mercury and Moon fits her description of how she used to write. She would rent a hotel room for the morning and lie in bed with just her notebook, some sherry and a deck of cards to play solitaire. She used the combination of solitude, sherry and solitaire to get into a kind of receptive trance state where her past became very real to her and she could re-enter it, and she would then write from that state of consciousness.

I think that reverie is a good reflection of the Moon and Mercury being averse, but having the antiscia connection, meaning it is outside of her direct conscious control, but she could get at it sideways through trance. She is practicing her own particular creative form of self hypnosis or trance work.

Angelou had very high reverence for the power of words to create - Mercury conjunct the exalted, revered Venus. Words have power, so being a poet and writer is an act of creation for her, a magical act of alchemy. She created the self she wanted to be by transmuting herself in her writing. She became the character she created, and we know Maya Angelou through her art.

Mars

Mars is the most difficult planet in Angelou's chart and it is also the most angular planet, being within 3 degrees of the Descendant. Through house rulership Mars is linked to eighth, ninth, third and fourth houses, so we have connections between the suffering caused by Mars and her family and relatives, and how dealing with those affected her philosophy.

Mars is strong by accidental dignity, being angular, direct and fast, but it is peregrine and out of sect, and it is dominated by the other malefic, Saturn.

At age 7 on a visit to her mother, Angelou was raped by her mother's boyfriend. She talked about the rape and who did it with her relatives, and a few days later the rapist was killed, probably by one of her uncles. Later in life she related that she stopped speaking because she was convinced her speaking had killed the man who raped her. The entire experience was so traumatic that she was silent for around five years.

Looking at her long period of silence after the rape, note that Mercury is in detriment and fall, in the eighth house of silent suffering. Note also that fall means not being listened to, which could equally well mean, not speaking. It is during that period of verbal silence that she developed her particular artistic perception and sensitivity.

We noted that she was convinced that her speaking had killed the man who raped her. This ties in with her lifetime belief in the power of words to directly shape the world. She had a very strong reverence for the power of words, and this experience of the trauma of rape and death is a core experience in giving her that conviction.

Mars in the seventh house is also linked to the instability of her marriage and other relationships with men. Her one child was born from a high school affair, and her early marriage to a Greek sailor fell apart after around three years.

Saturn

The other malefic, Saturn, is in the fifth house in Sagittarius. It has dignity by triplicity but it is also retrograde. Saturn rules sixth house of illness along with ruling the seventh.

We have noted that she had no good long term relationships. The Lord of the seventh house is in the fifth house. She bore a child while in high school that she raised on her own, and at times this was a great burden for her. Saturn in the fifth house ruling the sixth house is related to her caring for her son's health problems, including nursing him for an extended period after a serious accident.

Along with Mars, I think we can also link this Saturn in the fifth house ruling the seventh house to the rape experience in her childhood.

On the positive side, this Saturn makes a trine with the Sun/Jupiter conjunction in the 9th house, and both Sun and Jupiter receive Saturn. She was able to take all of her difficulties and misfortune and work with them.

Neptune

Note Neptune is the rising planet, conjunct the Ascendant by 3 degrees.

Given what we have said about Maya Angelou being her own created character, I think this Neptune placement is very apt. The Ascendant and Neptune are in Leo, ruled by the Sun. Much of her public persona was created through her writing. She is her own greatest fictional creation. Neptune on the Ascendant connects to Sun and Jupiter in the ninth house of publishing and writing.

We also see Neptune rising in the charts of the writer Jane Austen, and the actress Marilyn Monroe. Both are involved with fictional and artistic creation of a world and a character. We seem them only through their art created persona, in writing or on film.

Neptune is in a tight opposition with the malefic Mars in her seventh house on the Ascendant/Descendant axis. These are the two most angular planets, so they are important. Her re-creation of herself through writing is her response to the misfortune represented here by Mars.

Her name at birth was Marguerite Johnson, and she took the stage name Maya Angelou for a dance act after her second marriage to a Greek sailor. Neptune fits her creating a different identity with a different name, one associated in her mind with the ocean. It is also curious that her chosen first name, Maya, connotes illusion or fantasy, a meaning associated with the planet Neptune.

There are other associations with the malefic Mars in the seventh house of close relationships.

Angelou was close friends with Malcolm X, and began working with him shortly before Malcolm was killed. This was a devastating loss.

Angelou later became close friends with Martin Luther King and worked with him. *Martin Luther King was assassinated on Maya Angelou's birthday*, April 4, 1968, and after that she did not celebrate her birthday, but sent a card to King's widow.

This is Maya Angelou's solar return for the day Martin Luther King was shot and killed.

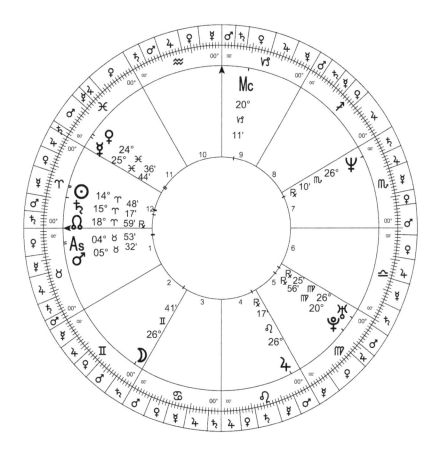

The malefic Mars, Lord of the twelfth house, is in detriment in Taurus and sitting right on the Ascendant. Mars also rules the seventh house of close partners and enemies. The Sun is in Aries in the twelfth house of hidden enemies, applying to a tight conjunction to Saturn in his fall in Aries. Sun exalted in the twelfth house moving to conjunction with Saturn in fall is an apt and touching metaphor for the fall of a great man she loved and admired.

Elizabeth Kubler Ross

In this example I want to focus on one planet that is about to station and change direction. Change of direction is an important change of dignity condition, and the station itself is a time of extra focus and importance.

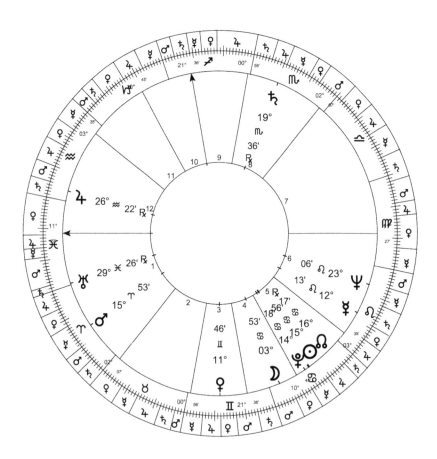

Elisabeth Kubler-Ross, July 8, 1926, 10:45 PM, Zurich, Switzerland. Rodden Rating A. Placidus houses.

Mars in Aries is in his rulership in Aries in the first house. Mars in the first house rules the eighth house, which is the first link we see between identity and death for her.

Saturn is the most debilitated planet, being peregrine, retrograde, and out of sect in the eighth house, and Saturn rules the eleventh and twelfth houses.

Saturn is far more influential in this chart than it looks at first glance. The Sun is within three and a half degrees of an exact trine to Saturn which means Saturn is nearing its second station.

Also note that Saturn is in mutual reception by bound with Jupiter in the twelfth house, and Saturn also rules Jupiter. Dignity by bound connotes implementation. This shows an eighth to twelfth house connection between death and places like hospitals and other places of confinement.

Looking in the ephemeris, around age 16 by secondary progression would be the time of Saturn's second station. Progressed planets changing direction are always major markers for a shift in a person's life. With a slow moving planet like Saturn, which slows to an almost complete stop for a couple of weeks, the effect of that station would be felt for years in the progressions, and dominate and entire period of life.

Kubler Ross turned 16 in 1942, in Europe in the middle of the Second World War. The following description from bio.com talks about those years.

> *Defying her family, Kübler-Ross left home at the age of 16 and worked a series of jobs. She also served as a volunteer during World War II, helping out in hospitals and caring for refugees. After the war, Kübler-Ross volunteered to help in numerous war-torn communities. She was profoundly affected by a visit to the Maidanek concentration camp in Poland and the images of hundreds of butterflies carved into some of the walls there. To Kübler-Ross, the butterflies— these final works of art by those facing death—stayed with her for years and influenced her thinking about the end of life.*

That pivotal set of experiences coincides with the progressed second station of Saturn. There is the intense combination of eighth house death in twelfth house places of confinement like refugee camps and Nazi concentration camps. This core set of experiences from Saturn's second station defined the agenda of the rest of her life.

Later in her life we see a sixth to twelfth house connection in a growing interest in the occult, especially contacting the dead.

Angela Davis

Angela Davis is a civil rights activist, feminist, philosopher, professor, and writer, and her life is consistent with her philosophy. The chart is a good example of a focus and coordination between planets, shown by their aspects, dignities and mutual reception. The energy of the chart all moves in a single direction.

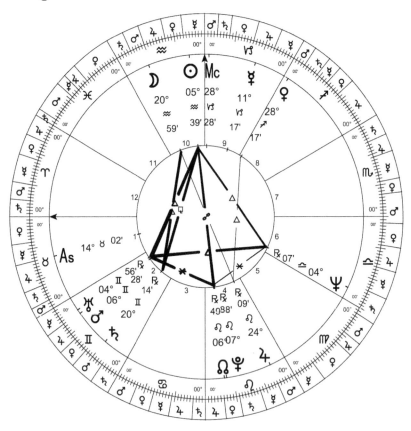

Angela Yvonne Davis, January 26, 1944, 12:30 PM (War Time), Birmingham, Alabama. Rodden Rating AA.

The focus of the chart is the most angular planet, the Sun, which is in Aquarius up in the tenth house, about seven degrees from the Capricorn midheaven. By dignity the Sun is dominated by Saturn (rulership, triplicity) and Mercury (triplicity and face). Keep the Sun's domination by Saturn and Mercury in mind when we examine those two planets.

Along with being angular the Sun is tightly conjunct the South Node by around a degree. Traditionally the South Node is considered of the nature of Saturn, and here I think it gives the Sun a self-giving, self-effacing quality. Combine this with the domination by Saturn in the fixed air sign Aquarius and you get a person who is driven by a strong sense of duty and obligation and by her ideals, her philosophy, which has a Saturnian rigid, fixed air quality. She is a high idealist whose life is dominated by her philosophy.

Mercury is in Capricorn in the ninth house of philosophy and teaching, and Mercury has two major mutual receptions that underline the importance of this planet. Saturn and Mercury have mutual reception by rulership, and Mercury and Saturn together are co-dispositors with all of the other planets tracing their rulership back to these two. Mercury in the ninth house is evident in her life, with Davis being a university professor and writer. The ninth house association with travel and foreign countries also fits - Davis traveled widely, and attended school at the Sorbonne in France, where she studied with Herbert Marcuse. In her later life she also traveled, lectured and taught all over the world.

In addition to the Saturn/Mercury connection, Mercury and Mars have mixed major mutual reception, rulership to exaltation. Both Mars and Saturn are in Gemini and are applying to conjunction, so those two together provide a lot of the tension and energy that drives this chart. Mars and Uranus are both trine the Sun by degree, and Saturn is trine the Sun by whole sign. This shows another way that Mars and Saturn dominate the expression of the angular Sun at the Midheaven.

Mars is far more important than it looks at first glance. Along with the Mercury/Mars reception Mars is also in mutual reception with Jupiter by both term and face.

Essential Dignities							
Pl	Ruler	Exalt	Tripl	Term	Face	Detri	Fall
☉	♄	--	♄☿♃	☿	♀	☉ -	--
☽	♄	--	♄☿♃	♂	☽ +	☉	--
☿	♄ m	♂	♀☽♂	♃	♂	☽	♃
♀	♃	☋	☉♃♄	♂	♄	☿	--
♂	☿	☊	♄☿♃	♃ m	♃ m	♃	--
♃	☉	--	☉♃♄ +	♂ m	♂ m	♄	--
♄	☿ m	☊	♄☿♃ +	♂	☉	♃	--
☊	☉	--	☉♃♄	♀	♄	♄	--
⊗	♀	☽	♀☽♂	♂	♄	♂	--
As	♀	☽	♀☽♂	♃	☽	♂	--
Mc	♄	♂	♀☽♂	♂	☉	☽	♃
☋	♄	--	♄☿♃	☿	♀	☉	--

Looking at overall dignity Mars also dominates the terms, with the Moon, Venus, Jupiter, Saturn and the Midheaven all working in his terms. Mars is the almuten of the Capricorn Midheaven, having dignity there by exaltation, triplicity and face. And finally, Mars is the rising planet conjunct the outer planet Uranus. Mars conjunct Uranus very aptly depicts her public image as a revolutionary and a radical philosopher.

Mars is the out of sect malefic, the planet likely to cause her the most trouble. It rules her seventh house of open enemies, and the twelfth house of hidden enemies and self-sacrifice.

The most famous incident of her life, that brought her to public notoriety, ties together these associations. Davis was drawn to championing the cause of black prisoners (twelfth house of prison, radical philosophy). Davis grew particularly attached to a young revolutionary, George Jackson, one of the Soledad Brothers, and she worked to help build a mass movement to free the Soledad Brothers who were facing a murder charge inside Soledad Prison. During an escape attempt, Jackson's brother Jonathan was among four persons killed, along with the trial judge from the Hall of Justice in Marin County, California. After that incident Angela

Davis was suspected of complicity, and Davis became one of the FBI's Ten Most Wanted criminals. Davis hit the headlines after she was accused of being involved in the planning and alleged kidnapping of three San Quentin prisoners, and of supplying the gun that killed four people during the incident.

After going into hiding, Davis was arrested. Her high visibility trial sparked massive public reaction and support, and the movement to Free Angela Davis received worldwide visibility. She was eventually acquitted of the charges. After that incident, and the publication of her autobiography telling the story, she became a world recognized radical political figure. All of her work after that, including work on (twelfth house) prison reform, grew from that incident.

Mars ruling seventh (public enemy) and twelfth (prison, going in to hiding) houses, Uranus, Saturn, trine the Sun in the tenth house, cooperating with Mercury in the ninth (public trial) house. All of the symbolism ties together in that incident.

Now back to the chart.

Mars is applying to conjunction with Saturn, and there is mixed mutual minor reception between them - Mars is in triplicity of Saturn, and Saturn is in terms of Mars. There is enormous pressure with the two malefics in conjunction, and the minor reception helps the two of them work together.

It is worth noting the elemental balance. Six of the planets are in air signs, three in Fire, and just one planet, Mercury, is in earth. The predominant element is air supported by fire, with very little to temper or moderate it. This fits with her being a revolutionary philosopher and professor with radical ideals.

There is a tight grand trine in air including the Sun in Aquarius, Neptune in Libra, Mars and Uranus in Gemini - again we see the marks of a highly individualistic, idealistic and radical philosopher. If you allow for a wider orb the trine includes the Moon and Saturn also, so that one highly integrated configuration has half of the planets in her chart including the two most dominant planets, Saturn and Mars.

The Sun is highly visible and angular in the tenth house in detriment, in the fixed air sign Aquarius, dominated by Saturn (rulership, triplicity) and Mercury (triplicity and term). The Sun is conjunct the South Node, which I think relates to her identity and ethic of self-sacrifice. Her personal life was subordinate to her values and her philosophy.

Running through the center of the grand trine there is an opposition along the nodal axis between the Moon, Sun and South node, all of which are highly visible in the tenth house, and Jupiter, Pluto and the North Node at the bottom of the chart. (This shape is called a kite in modern astrology.) The opposition is angular along the Midheaven/IC axis. This highly charged opposition is integrated and expressed through the trine/sextile aspect to the Uranus/Mars/Saturn cluster in Gemini - again, highlighting Saturn and Mars.

The chart is a good example of what happens when all of the planets cohere with a common focus, to all work in a common direction.

Conclusion - It Depends...

I want to conclude this book on using the dignities by re-emphasizing something I stated earlier about using the Cheate Sheete to evaluate a chart.

Don't get hung up on the scoring.

The Cheate Sheete is training you in a process of what to scan for in a chart. If you use it with any consistency, you will start to recognize that evaluating the condition and action of a planet involves many more conditions than you would think at first glance.

You will also find yourself trying to evaluate quite a few borderline conditions, to figure out if you should apply the point value or not. For instance, take a situation where you see Saturn is in an applying square to the Sun with an orb of just over two degrees. Should you apply the minus points to the Sun for squaring a malefic? Well, let's see - what condition is the Sun in, what condition is Saturn, is there any reception between them, is Saturn direct or retrograde, and so on.

Should you apply the negative points? It depends... and noticing the square, and all of those other factors, is precisely the point of the exercise. The meaning of that Saturn Sun square is much more complex than you'd think.

Take another case - I will use Saturn in my own chart as an example. I have a night chart, so Saturn is the out of sect malefic, and the ruler of my Ascendant, Capricorn. On top of that Saturn is retrograde, so this should be really bad, right?.. But on the other hand Saturn is exalted in Libra, which means it also has dignity by triplicity in an air sign. Saturn also has a very nice major mutual reception with Venus in Aquarius, the benefic of night charts, and they aspect each other by trine. And then there's the Saturn Jupiter opposition - but both planets have dignity, and there is some reception between them... and so on.

So, does the out of sect malefic Saturn have a negative effect in my chart? It depends... and in this case all of those positive points do a lot to mitigate Saturn's effect, so that even the difficulties that Saturn causes end up having positive sides to them in the long run - and positive effects in the long run is a characteristically Saturnine effect.

Mars is retrograde - is that bad? It depends...

Venus is combust - is that bad? It depends...

Sun is exalted in Aries - that's really good, right? It depends...

I think you will find that, as you use the various dignities and debilities in your chart work, that their meaning will become more subtle and complex. Using the dignities is all about noticing that complex mixture of factors, the 'it depends' part of chart reading. Charts will become much more multi-dimensional and subtle, and you will notice details you had never realized were there.

Having a basic understanding of the framework of dignities and debilities will also help you in exploring traditional astrology texts. It will help to give you an understanding of what they are talking about when they describe the effects of the planets in what seem to be such extreme ways. The dignities give a framework to organize the interpretations.

When you know about dignity and debility, reading the old texts is a lot more fun, and makes a lot more sense. I encourage you to explore the rich heritage of traditional astrology, and draw your own conclusions.

The dignities and debilities add a very rich and rewarding set of tools to your astrological repertoire. Enjoy using them.

Appendix: Cheate Sheetes and Dignity Tables

On the following pages you will find the Cheate Sheete scoring system in tabular reference form.

The first table, **William Lilly's Cheate Sheete**, is taken from Lilly's Table of Fortitudes and Debilities in *Christian Astrology*.

The second table, **Charlie's New Improved Cheate Sheete** is my own, slightly modified system, where I adjusted the scoring for some items and added a few other conditions that I find very important.

You may likely find that you wish to make your own adjustments to the system based on your own experience.

The third is a table of all of the **Essential Dignities**.

William Lilly's Cheate Sheete

A ready table whereby to examine the *fortitudes* and *debilities* of the Planets

ESSENTIAL DIGNITIES	RATING	ESSENTIAL DEBILITIES	RATING
Rulership (Domicile)	5	Detriment	-5
Exaltation	4	Fall	-4
Triplicity	3		
Term	2	Peregrine	-5
Face	1		
Rulership and Exaltation are considered MAJOR; Triplicity, Term and Face are considered MINOR.			
Mutual Reception			
by Rulership	5		
by Exaltation	4		
etc			

ACCIDENTAL DIGNITIES		ACCIDENTAL DEBILITIES	
Relative House Strength		**Relative House Strength**	
In MC or ASC	5	In 12th house	-5
In 7th 4th or 11th house	4	In 8th or 6th houses	-4
In 2nd or 5th house	3	*(note: these houses do not*	
In 9th house	2	*aspect or behold the ASC.)*	
In 3rd house	1		
Direct in motion (not ☉ or ☽)	4	Retrograde	-5
Swift in motion	2	Slow in motion	-2
Important Aspects		**Important Aspects**	
partile ☌ ♃ or ♀	5	partile ☌ ♄ or ♂	-5
partile ☌ ☊	4	partile ☌ ☋	-4
partile △ ♃ or ♀	4	partile △ ♄ or ♂	-4
partile ✷ ♃ or ♀	3	partile ✷ ♄ or ♂	-3
Beseiged by ♃ or ♀	5	Beseiged by ♄ or ♂	-5
Free from combustion or sunbeams	5	Combust (8° orb)	-5
Cazimi (heart of ☉)	5	Under the sunbeams (17°)	-4
☽ Occidental (increasing)	2	☽ Oriental (decreasing)	-2
♄ ♃ ♂ oriental	2	♄ ♃ ♂ occidental	-2
♀ ☿ occidental	2	♀ ☿ oriental	-2
☌ Regulus (29 ♌)	6	☌ Caput Algol (26 ♉)	-5
☌ Spica (23 ♎)	5		

Charlie's Cheate Sheete

A new, improved table whereby to examine the fortitudes and debilities of the Planets

ESSENTIAL DIGNITIES	RATING	ESSENTIAL DEBILITIES	RATING
Rulership (Domicile)	5	Detriment	-5
Exaltation	4	Fall	-4
Term	3		
Triplicity	2	Peregrine	-3
Face	1		
Mutual Reception			
by Rulership	5		
by Exaltation	4		
(etc - include major mixed receptions)			
In Sect	3	Out of Sect	-3

ACCIDENTAL DIGNITIES		ACCIDENTAL DEBILITIES	
Relative House Strength		**Relative House Strength**	
In MC or ASC	5	In 12th house	-5
In 7th 4th or 11th house	4	In 8th or 6th houses	-4
In 2nd or 5th house	3	*(note: these houses do not*	
In 9th house	2	*aspect or behold the ASC.)*	
In 3rd house	1		
Direct in motion (not ☉ or ☽)	4	Retrograde	-5
Swift in motion	2	Slow in motion	-2
Important Aspects		**Important Aspects**	
close ☌ ♃ or ♀	5	close ☌ ♄ or ♂	-5
close ☌ ☊	4	close ☌ ☋	-4
close △ ♃ or ♀	4	close ☍ ♄ or ♂	-4
close ✳ ♃ or ♀	3	close □ ♄ or ♂	-3
(2° applying, 1° separating)			
Beseiged by ♃ or ♀	5	Beseiged by ♄ or ♂	-5
Antiscia to ♃ or ♀	5	Antiscia or Contrantiscia to ♄ or ♂	-5
Free from combustion or sunbeams	5	Combust (7° orb)	-5
Cazimi (heart of ☉)	5	Under the sunbeams (17°)	-4
Heliacal Rising	5	Heliacal Setting	-5
☽ Occidental (increasing)	2	☽ Oriental (decreasing)	-2
♄ ♃ ♂ oriental	2	♄ ♃ ♂ occidental	-2
♀ ☿ occidental	2	♀ ☿ oriental	-2
☌ Regulus (29 ♌) 6° orb	6	☌ Caput Algol (26 ♉) 6° orb	-5
☌ Spica (23 ♎) 6° orb	5		

Tables of Essential Dignities

Sign	Ruler	Detriment	Exaltation	Fall	Triplicity Day	Night	Partner	Face 0-9	10-19	20-29
♈	♂	♀	☉	♄	☉	♃	♄	♂	☉	♀
♉	♀	♂	☽		♀	☽	♂	☿	☽	♄
♊	☿	♃			♄	☿	♃	♃	♂	☉
♋	☽	♄	♃	♂	♀	♂	☽	♀	☿	☽
♌	☉	♄			☉	♃	♄	♄	♃	♂
♍	☿	♃	☿	♀	♀	☽	♂	☉	♀	☿
♎	♀	♂	♄	☉	♄	☿	♃	☽	♄	♃
♏	♂	♀		☽	♀	♂	☽	♂	☉	♀
♐	♃	☿			☉	♃	♄	☿	☽	♄
♑	♄	☽	♂	♃	♀	☽	♂	♃	♂	☉
♒	♄	☉			♄	☿	♃	♀	☿	☽
♓	♃	☿	♀	☿	♀	♂	☽	♄	♃	♂

Bounds or Terms

♈	0	♃	6	♀	12	☿	20	♂	25	♄
♉	0	♀	8	☿	14	♃	22	♄	27	♂
♊	0	☿	6	♃	12	♀	17	♂	24	♄
♋	0	♂	7	♀	13	☿	18	♃	26	♄
♌	0	♃	6	♀	11	♄	18	☿	24	♂
♍	0	☿	7	♀	17	♃	21	♂	28	♄
♎	0	♄	6	☿	14	♃	21	♀	28	♂
♏	0	♂	7	♀	11	☿	19	♃	24	♄
♐	0	♃	12	♀	17	☿	21	♄	26	♂
♑	0	☿	7	♃	14	♀	22	♄	26	♂
♒	0	☿	7	♀	13	♃	20	♂	25	♄
♓	0	♀	12	♃	16	☿	19	♂	28	♄

The degree in the term table is the degree that bound starts.
For instance, Venus term in Aries begins at 6 degrees.

Bibliography

Al-Biruni, **The Book of Instructions in the Elements of the Art of Astrology**. Translation by R. Ramsay Wright. Edited by David R. Roell. Maryland, Astrology Classics, 2006.

Dykes, Benjamin N. Ph. D., translator. **Bonatti On Basic Astrology**: *Treatises 1-3 of Guido Bonatti's Book of Astronomy*. Minneapolis, Cazimi Press, 2010.

_____**Bonatti's 146 Considerations**: *Treatise 5 of Guido Bonatti's Book of Astronomy*. Minneapolis, Cazimi Press, 2010.

_____**Bonatti On Horary**: *Treatise 6 of Guido Bonatti's Book of Astronomy*. Minneapolis, Cazimi Press, 2010.

_____ Dorotheus of Sidon, **Carmen Astrologicum**: The 'Umar al-Tabari Translation. 2017.

_____**Works of Sahl and Masha'Allah**. 2008.

Obert, Charles, **Introduction to Traditional Natal Astrology**. Almuten Press, 2015.

Ibn-Ezra, Avraham, **The Beginning of Wisdom**. Translated by Meira B. Epstein. Arhat Publications, 1998.

Lilly, William, **Christian Astrology, Books 1 & 2**. Edited by David R. Roell. Maryland, Astrology Classics, 2004.

Maternus, Julius Firmicus, **Mathesis**. Edited and Translated by James Herschel Holden M.S. Arizona, American Federation of Astrologers, 2011.

Paul of Alexandria, **Introduction to Astrology**. Translated by James Herschel Holden M.S. Arizona, American Federation of Astrologers, 2012.

Rhetorius the Egyptian, **Astrological Compendium Containing His Explanation and Narration of the Whole Art of Astrology**. Translated by James Herschel Holden M.S. Arizona, American Federation of Astrologers, 2009.

Sepharial, **The Manual of Astrology**. London, W. Foulsham & Co. Ltd., 1979

Vettius Valens, **Anthology**. The translation by Mark T. Riley is available at this URL - http://www.csus.edu/indiv/r/rileymt/Vettius%20Valens%20entire.pdf

CPSIA information can be obtained
at www.ICGtesting.com
Printed in the USA
BVHW011931130619
550806BV00047B/1042/P